Brenda Bly:
Teen Detective

A musical

Book and lyrics by Kevin Hammonds
Music by Charles Miller

Samuel French — London
www.samuelfrench-london.co.uk

FOR AMATEUR PRODUCTION ENQUIRIES

UNITED KINGDOM AND WORLD EXCLUDING NORTH AMERICA

plays@SamuelFrench-London.co.uk

020 7255 4302/01

Each title is subject to availability from Samuel French,

depending upon country of performance.

BRENDA BLY:
TEEN DETECTIVE

First produced by Glenn Lee and Fenton Gray for the London School of Musical Theatre at the Cochrane Theatre, London in August 2002.

The show was revised and subsequently produced by Glenn Lee at the Bridewell Theatre, London in August/ September 2003, with the following cast:

Brenda Bly	Cassidy Janson
Buddy Rogers	Joshua Dallas
Vera Van Strander	Ruth Madoc
Darcy	Jessica Robinson
Jo Jo	Holly Graham
Autumn	Laura Checkley
Stu	Richard Runnalls
Madeline	Melitsa Nicola
Cecil Sessile/Wally	Charles Shirvell
Bridget	Lisa Baird
Gidget	Sarah Annis
Candy	Collette Fraser

Director/Lighting Designer Fenton Gray
Choreographer Sam Spencer Lane
Musical Director Colin Billing
Designer Amy Jackson
Sound Designer Tony Gayle
Casting Director Graham Hubbard

ISBN 10 - 0 573 08128 X

ISBN 13 - 978 0 573 08128 6

CHARACTERS

Brenda Bly
Buddy Rogers
Vera Van Strander
Darcy
Jo Jo
Autumn
Stu
Madeline
Cecil Sessile
Wally
Bridget
Gidget
Candy
Nurse Wilder
Nurse Iris
Nurse Ivy
A Villain
A Mad Groundskeeper
A Cool Dude
Creepy Miss Jenkins

The action of the play takes place in and around The Whitney Ellis Private School For Girls, Florida, McFrostie's Soda Shop, and Van Strander's Remote Cabin In The Woods.

Time — 1958

CHARACTER DESCRIPTIONS

Brenda Bly is everybody's favourite teen detective: confident, charming and loyal. Her hair is perfectly coiffed, and she looks every bit the perfect teenager she strives to be. Even in peril, she manages to keep her cool.

Darcy is one of Brenda's best friends; pretty, a bit ditsy, and all pink and frills.

Jo Jo is Brenda's other best friend, a short-tempered, wise-cracking girl who is more interested in boys than following the rules.

Autumn is in charge of the end of term show and treats it as if it were an opening on Broadway. She is a very serious student and will not let anyone get in the way of her great opus.

Madeline is the French foreign exchange student. She wears her own school uniform, complete with beret.

Bridget and **Gidget** are twin sisters who used to be child stars with their own television show, but once they grew into their teens the show was dropped and they were sent back to private school, and the only thing that remains from their heyday is the identical red curly hair they unfortunately never grew out of. Desperate to revive her career, Bridget considers herself worldly, sophisticated, and extremely more talented than the others. She is wrong on all accounts. Gidget has been around the block more than most girls her age. She smokes, and is attracted to men from the wrong side of the tracks.

Vera Van Strander is the headmistress of the school, a no-nonsense woman in her mid-forties who suffers no fools, and is always quick to point out anyone's flaws. She is glamorous, but proper; sophisticated, but stern, with a wicked and sarcastic sense of humour that terrifies anyone in its path.

Cecil Sessile is the school security guard. He is a bumbling, self-important man in his mid forties. He is a cross between Phil Silvers and Don Knotts, always trying to elbow his way into any crisis, just in time to make matters even worse.

Buddy Rogers. He is a clean-cut, "All-American" Boy. Cocky and self-assured, but charming enough to get away with it. In short, he is the perfect match for Brenda Bly, and is madly in love with her.

Dr Sniffles. He is your typical smooth-talking, devilishly handsome doctor straight out of a daytime soap opera. His smile is bright and hypnotic. He blankly stares down at his armful of medical charts.

Stu. He is a cute, geeky, high-strung young man who doesn't like trouble, and gets even more nervous when he's around girls. '

Wally, a soda jerk.

Candy, a Whitney Ellis schoolgirl.

DOUBLING

Wally: the **Villain**, the **Mad Groundskeeper**, **Dr Sniffles** and the **Cool Dude.**
Nurse Wilder: Schoolgirl
Nurse Iris: Candy
Nurse Ivy: Creepy Miss Jenkins

The ideal casting uses the doubling above. It is possible to reduce the cast to twelve (M3 F9) by having the same actor play **Cecil Sessile, Wally** and all the small cameo roles (including **Creepy Miss Jenkins**). **Bridget** and **Gidget** would double as **Nurse Iris** and **Nurse Ivy; Nurse Wilder** would double as Candy. It is also possible to increase the cast size by having extra students in the company scenes.

SYNOPSIS OF SCENES AND MUSICAL NUMBERS

ACT I

1 **Prologue: Brenda Bly: Teen Detective** (Entire Company)

SCENE 1   Cape Canaveral/On The Bus/Whitney Ellis School For Girls Auditorium

2 **Times Like These** (Students of Whitney Ellis School)

SCENE 2   On the set of "Rocket Girl"

3 **Next Stop The Moon** (Darcy, Jo Jo and "Rocket Girl" cast)

4 **Next Stop The Moon: Reprise** (Darcy)

5 **I Always Get My Man** (Brenda Bly)

SCENE 3   The Hospital

6 **A Girl Like Me**   (Darcy, Autumn, Nurse Wilder, Nurse Iris, Nurse Ivy and Dr Sniffles)

SCENE 4   Backstage

7 **Find Me That Man** (Van Strander and Cecil)

SCENE 5   Onstage

8 **Showbiz** (Autumn and "Rocket Girl" cast)

SCENE 6   The Prop Room

9 **Cha Cha Cha** (Brenda and Buddy)

SCENE 7   The Costume Store

10 **I Always Get My Man: Reprise** (Jo Jo)

11 **Jo Jo's Undercover** (Jo Jo)

SCENE 8   The Prop Room

12 **I Always Get My Man: Reprise** (Van Strander)

13 **A Thief In The Night** (Brenda and Buddy)

ACT II

Scores, vocal books, orchestral parts and a demo music CD for
BRENDA BLY: TEEN DETECTIVE
are on hire from Samuel French Ltd

ACT 1

PROLOGUE

The back wall of the stage has the words "Whitney Ellis Private School for Girls" painted across the top of it. DS of this is a set of curtains with a centre opening; these divide the stage into US and DS areas. US of these curtains is a stand-alone flat painted to resemble a cliff; this flat has a ladder behind it

There is a girl's ear-piercing scream and the House Lights snap out

The front curtains open. The stage is in darkness and the US curtains are open. Brenda Bly is standing L, reaching up and hanging on to the top of the flat, as if hanging from the cliff. The Villain stands on the ladder behind the cliff flat, visible from the waist up, as if standing on the cliff. He looks down on Brenda

Music No. 1: Prologue: Brenda Bly: Teen Detective (*Entire company*)

The Lights come up on the US area

Villain Not so smart now, are you Brenda Bly?

Brenda You'll never get away with this.

Villain But I have gotten away with it. Only how did you figure it out?

Brenda Quite simple really. You're not the first jewel thief to hide diamonds in a paper maché clock.

Villain Too bad your knowledge of paper maché can't help you out of this jam.

Brenda That's where you're wrong. The gun you're holding is paper maché.

Villain Damn!

Brenda That grassy knoll you're standing on is paper maché.

Villain Damn!

Brenda However, the pit beneath it is absolutely real.

Villain Ahhh!!!!

The Villain drops behind the flat in slow motion

The US curtains close and the US Lights cross-fade to the DS area

The whole cast, except Brenda, Darcy and Creepy Miss Jenkins, enters DS *dressed in trench coats and fedoras and carrying flashlights*

All (*singing*)	There's danger in the air
	And trouble round the bend
	Just who, what, when and where
	Will all this madness end
Girls	The only one with answers to our query
Boys	With gorgeous hair and always thorough theory
All	Private eye and so effective
	Brenda Bly
	Teen Detective

The Lights cross-fade to the US *area. The* US *curtains open to reveal a haunted house setting. Brenda, with Darcy hiding behind her, faces Creepy Miss Jenkins who is disguised as a sheeted ghost and trying to spook them from across the room*

During the following, Jo Jo exits from the DS *area*

Creepy Miss Jenkins (*as a ghost*) Woooooo! Woooooo!
Darcy Brenda, the ghost of Bernard Mansion!
Brenda That's no ghost, Darcy. That's creepy Miss Jenkins from next door!

Brenda pulls the sheet off the ghost to reveal Creepy Miss Jenkins

Creepy Miss Jenkins You pesky kids! But how could you possibly know?
Brenda The real Lady Bernard died in her sleep. Which immediately led me to notice the obvious. If you were the actual ghost of Bernard Mansion, you'd be wearing no shoes!

The US *curtains close on Darcy, Brenda and Creepy Miss Jenkins and the Lights cross-fade to the* DS *area*

All (*singing*)	A culprit on the loose
	A low life on the lam
	A very good excuse
	To leave this place and scram
	But never fear, there's no need to feel danger
	We've got a gal who'll stop that unknown stranger
	Never shy and not defective
	Brenda Bly
	Teen Detective

No other snoop can swoop and scoop
A troupe of gangsters
There's not a lad gone bad or mad she hasn't stopped
You'll never name a better gumshoe
On land or sea or wheels
She'll track each scum down to their scum shoe
And do it all in heels

The Lights cross-fade to the US *area. The* US *curtains open on a setting that suggests a deserted warehouse. Brenda and Darcy are tied together back to back with Jo Jo on a wooden crate. A Mad Groundskeeper hovers above them with a shovel*

Mad Groundskeeper You almost stopped me from carrying out my dastardly plan, Brenda Bly. But I'll be ding-danged if I let you re-open this amusement park!

Jo Jo This is it, isn't it Brenda Bly? I knew I'd die before I kissed a man!

Brenda Don't cash in your lipstick just yet, Jo Jo. I've managed to cut the ropes with a file I fashioned from my Girl Scout pin and locket.

Darcy So what are we waiting for?

Brenda The perfect music. Now!

Brenda jumps up, followed by Jo Jo and Darcy. In slow motion, they fight the Mad Groundskeeper and eventually leave him lying motionless on the floor

The Lights cross-fade back to the DS *area and the* US *curtains close*

All (*singing*)   If danger in the air
                          Sneaks up to trump your ace
                          Just send up any flare
                          And Brenda's on the case
                          She's smart and slim in every way a winner
                          She'll save the day and be back home for dinner

The US *curtains open. Brenda steps down from the* US *area and joins the group* DS. *Darcy and Jo Jo move* UR *and* UL *respectively, cheering on their famous friend*

	Get the guy
Brenda	That's *my* objective
All	Brenda Bly
	Teen Detective

Black-out

Music No. 1a: Prologue Tag

Everyone except Brenda Bly exits

The Lights come up DS

The Mad Groundskeeper enters DS. *He is hog tied, and desperately trying to escape, hopping across the stage*

Brenda Bly watches, hands on hips, and shakes her finger disapprovingly at the Mad Groundskeeper. She grabs the end of the rope and hangs on tight. Resigned, the Mad Groundskeeper turns, and hops towards the exit with Brenda right behind him

The US *curtains open fully as Brenda and the Mad Groundskeeper head off, revealing a bare stage*

They exit

SCENE 1

Cape Canaveral / On The Bus / Whitney Ellis Private School for Girls Auditorium

Music No. 2: Times Like These (*Students of Whitney Ellis*)

The Visitor's Center at Cape Canaveral

A freestanding sign is placed DR: *it reads:' "Welcome to Cape Canaveral Visitors' Center"*

The Lights come up brightly over the whole stage. The students of Whitney Ellis School for Girls are on a field trip. As the song begins, the girls (among them Autumn, Jo Jo, Darcy, Madeline, Bridget, Gidget and Candy) pour on to the stage (as if coming out of the Visitors' Center) armed with souvenirs, such as rocket models, T-shirts and posters. Darcy also has a camera with a flashgun

Girls (*singing*)   Sha-do-wa-she-wop
                    Sha-do-wa-she-wop
                    Isn't it great
                    Clearly the best
                    Looking at us who won't be impressed

	Sha-do-wa-she-wop
	To be-bop
	In times like these
	Sha-do-wa-she-wop
	Sha-do-wa-she-wop
Autumn	Isn't it swell
	Aren't we the most
Jo Jo	Hear Elvis Presley from coast to coast
Girls	Sha-do-wa-she-wop
	To be-bop
	In times like these
	Sha-do-wa-she-wop
	Sha-do-wa-she-wop
Autumn	We're gonna win soon
	In our race to the moon
	There's fin'lly a polio vaccine.
Darcy ⎤	We hear Disneyland
Jo Jo ⎦	Is so perfect and grand
Bridget	And I'm certain to wed Jimmy Dean
Gidget	I'll beat ya to it
Girls	Isn't it hip
Bridget	Really too too
Girls	Our latest fashion – our greatest do
	Sha-do-wa-she-wop
	To be-bop
	In times like these

Brenda enters

Brenda (*speaking*) OK, ladies. I've enjoyed this field trip as much as anyone, but I think it's time we get back to school.
Autumn Brenda, thank you so much for driving us to Cape Canaveral.
Brenda It was my pleasure.
Autumn Thank goodness you're the one girl in the entire school who has her driver license.
Darcy And knows how to drive a school bus.
Brenda I knew that summer course in public transport would come in handy. All aboard!

The Lights change for a bus trip. During the following, the girls roll on three sets of bus seats (on the first of which is pre-set a steering wheel) and create the school bus. They all get on board with Brenda Bly at the front, driving with the wheel. The Visitors' Center sign is removed

Girls	Isn't it keen
	Excellence shows
	Wearin' our hair
	In Marilyn Monroes
	Sha-do-wa-she-wop
	To be-bop
	In times like these
	Sha-do-wa-she-wop
	Sha-do-wa-she-wop
	Old folks think change
	Is unsettling and strange
	But that's when the place starts to swing
Brenda	We're starting to date
	And this girl, she can't wait
	To see what the Sixties might bring
Girls	The Sixties might bring
	The Sixties might bring
	The Sixties might bring

The girls arrive back at school. They are on stage in the auditorium of The Whitney Ellis Private School for Girls, where a show is obviously in rehearsal

The Lights change to a suitable setting for the school stage. During the following, the bus seats are wheeled off stage. A rack of costumes and a cut-out flat of a rocket ship (facing US and behind the line of the US curtains) are wheeled on. The US curtains are edged in to suggest the auditorium's curtains

Isn't it fun (Fun!)
Isn't it great (Great!)
Don't ya just love nineteen fifty-eight
Sha-do-wa-she-wop
To be-bop
In times like these
So take this time and clock it
We're soaring in a rocket
We're gonna rock it and clock it
In times like these
We're gonna rock it and clock it
In times like these
We're gonna rock it and clock it
In times like
These!

At the end of the song, the girls pose for a picture that Darcy is taking. They smile and freeze as the flash goes off

Brenda runs off with the bus keys

During the following, Madeline, the French Foreign Exchange student, grins inanely, unable to understand a word anyone is saying

Autumn (*with great authority*) Ladies, the field trip to Cape Canaveral was great fun, but let's not forget why we went in the first place. Our fall musical is only days away from opening night. We must get back to rehearsal.

Darcy One second, Autumn. One last group picture.

Autumn Darcy, really, we've got a great responsibility before us. I am the first student in the history of Whitney Ellis Private School for Girls to ever write, direct, produce and make costumes for her very own production: *Rocket Girl, The Musical!*

Darcy Jo Jo, be sure to thank your father again. Who knew the space programme was so interesting?

Autumn I knew! In fact, I wrote a musical about it. Anyone care to get back to it?

Darcy I especially liked meeting the astronauts. Did you see how that one astronaut couldn't take his eyes off of me?

Jo Jo That's because you were standing on his oxygen hose.

Autumn takes a military uniform from the rack and hands it to Jo Jo

Autumn Here, try this on.

Jo Jo What is it?

Autumn It's your costume.

Jo Jo You gotta be kidding me. You won't be able to see my figure at all.

Autumn That's the way it should be. You're playing General Flavaven.

Jo Jo Autumn, I am in my prime. I wake up in the morning and I find things that weren't there the night before. I'd like a chance to display the goods.

Autumn It's an *all-girls* school. Somebody's got to play the man. So, if you're done complaining, I'd like to start from the top. (*She moves* US *and signals off to have the curtains closed*)

The US *curtains close and the Lights go down on the* US *area*

Darcy Just one more picture. I've got to use up the rest of the film. I got some very interesting pictures this afternoon. I want to run out and get them developed.

Madeline runs forward excitedly and takes the camera from Darcy

Madeline Bonjour!
Darcy It's OK, Madeline. I'll take the picture.

Madeline shakes her head and directs Darcy to get in the group. Autumn takes the camera from Madeline

Autumn I'll take it, Madeline. It'll be nice to have the entire company in the shot.
Jo Jo Frenchy isn't in the show. She doesn't know a kick line from a corkscrew.
Autumn She's our spotlight operator.
Jo Jo You've gotta be kidding!

Autumn takes hold of Madeline and moves her to the group. The rest of the girls gather around

Autumn Isn't part of a foreign exchange programme to immerse yourself in your new homeland's culture?
Jo Jo That's easy for you to say. She isn't your roommate, immersing herself into everything you own. *Bonjour! Bonjour!*
Autumn Say cheese!
Girls Cheese!
Madeline *Fromage!*

Autumn takes the picture. The group breaks up

Autumn Now, can we please get on with rehearsal?

Everyone exits but Jo Jo, Madeline and Autumn

Madeline, you're the spotlight operator. Remember?
Madeline *Bonjour!*
Autumn Spotlight.
Jo Jo I'll take her.

Jo Jo drags Madeline towards the exit

Hey, if this is a foreign exchange programme, how come I'm not in France?
Madeline *Bonjour.*
Jo Jo Shut up.

They exit

Autumn All right, ladies. From the top.

Music No. 3: Next Stop, the Moon (*"Rocket Girl" cast*)

Reporters in a frenzy. Wives in tears. The race to the moon has begun and Rocket Girl is in the lead. Curtain!

SCENE 2

On the set of "Rocket Girl" : The Flight to the Moon

The US *curtains open and Lights come up on the* US *area. A sign saying "Rocket Girl: Inaugural Flight to the Moon" has been flown in. Bridget and Gidget are dressed as newspaper reporters. They are joined by other girls dressed as scientists with geeky glasses and clipboards. Everything is rather glamorous and has been slightly over-choreographed by Autumn, who stands at the side of the stage correcting any mistakes (of which there are a few)*

Bridget ⎫ **Gidget** ⎭	Stop the press You'll never guess The future we all face Now the time has fin'lly come To shoot to outer space We'll sail towards a brand new world That's bright and full of hope
Bridget	We're gonna see the galaxy
Gidget	We're gonna see the galaxy
Bridget ⎫ **Gidget** ⎭	Without a telescope
Autumn (*speaking*)	That's it girls. Busy, busy!
Girls (*singing*)	The USA did say one day The moon was in our reach Now that time has fin'lly come To practise what we preach Around the bend My starry friend It's up up and away
Bridget ⎫ **Girls** ⎭	We're gonna see the galaxy
Gidget ⎫ **Girls** ⎭	We're gonna see the galaxy
All	God bless the USA.

Jo Jo enters, now dressed as General Flavaven

Jo Jo (*speaking; reluctantly*) Ladies and Gentlemen, members of the press,
Mr President. I proudly give you Rocket Girl.
Girls (*singing*)   Ah! Ah!

*Darcy enters, dressed as Rocket Girl in a complete astronaut outfit. She
takes off her helmet and places it under her arm*

Darcy (*singing*)   On with my space suit
                        Off with a bang
                        I've packed my suitcase
                        Said goodbye to all the gang
                        An adventure of a lifetime
                        Is gonna happen soon
                        Buckle up, ladies
                        Next stop — the Moon
All   Out with the old bag
                        In with the new
Darcy   With all that weightlessness
                        I guess I'll eat for two
Darcy ⎤   And then every doubting Thomas
Girls ⎦   Will have to change his tune
Darcy   All aboard ladies
Girls   All aboard ladies
                        Next stop — the Moon

                        Way out past the wild blue yonder
                        You can keep your stinking cars
                        In our lunar ship we can sooner trip
                        Along the milky way and past the stars

*The rocket ship flat is turned to face the audience. Darcy moves behind the
rocket and the others bid Rocket Girl farewell with great fanfare*

                        Touch the big dipper
                        Say ciao to mirth (Ciao)
                        We're close to heaven while
                        The men are stuck on earth
                        An adventure of a lifetime
                        Is gonna happen soon

Darcy sticks her head out of the tiny rocket window

Darcy	All aboard, ladies
All	Ooooooh!
Darcy	Next stop — the Moon
All	One fine day
	The USA will sail beyond the stars! Stars! Stars!

They all freeze in a typical musical theatre pose. During the applause, Darcy crosses back to Autumn from behind the rocket

Autumn (*speaking*) God, I'm good.

Darcy You really are, Autumn. Top drawer.

Autumn Did you hear the way I rhymed lunar ship with sooner trip?

Van Strander (*off*) For God's sake someone kill me!

Autumn Miss Van Strander, is that you?

Vera Van Strander enters from the wings

Van Strander No, it's Florenz Ziegfield. Get this garbage off the stage.

Autumn But we've booked the stage for another hour.

Van Strander I am the headmistress of the Whitney Ellis Private School For Girls. I say how long you have the theatre booked for. And if you're not out of here in half an hour I'm shutting this show down.

Bridget But this is our chance to make a comeback.

Van Strander My dear, Hitler has a better chance of a comeback. If it's glamour and attention you crave, join Home Economics. You'll be sewing your own cocktail dresses by mid-term. (*She heads for the exit*) Half an hour!

Van Strander exits

Darcy Don't let Van Strander get you down, Autumn. You've written a wonderful play. It's very funny.

Autumn Funny? It's not supposed to be funny!

Bridget You have a Girl Scout from Encino going to the moon and opening her own hair salon.

Autumn It's political satire.

Gidget It's garbage!

Brenda Bly enters

Brenda Mission accomplished. (*She throws the bus keys to Autumn*) The school bus is parked, refuelled and for extra measure I changed the oil.

Autumn Thanks again for driving us, Brenda.

Brenda Don't mention it. It was my pleasure.
Autumn Great. Thanks again. Bye.

Autumn moves US *with Bridget and Gidget to continue rehearsing*

Brenda Bye? Don't I get to watch rehearsal? I'm dying to see it.
Darcy We'd love to have you watch, Brenda. But you must be incredibly busy. Don't you have to solve "The Case of the Agitated Attic"?
Brenda Oh, that tiny thing? Turned out to be a grumpy neighbour with a recording device and a bed sheet.
Jo Jo Brenda, no-one's gonna tell you the truth, so I'm just gonna let you have it. You're bad luck with a capital black cat. No-one wants you here.
Brenda I just want to help out, that's all.
Jo Jo You wanna help? Go home. Build a birdhouse for your father.
Brenda I already did.
Darcy Bake a cake.
Brenda It's cooling as we speak.
Jo Jo Make a dress.

Music No. 3a: Brenda's Dress

Brenda twirls around showing off her newly sewn dress

Jo Jo I don't know why I'm friends with you, I really don't.
Darcy (*to Brenda*) You're a smart girl. You have to notice that anytime you're around, something bad happens.
Brenda Now you're talking crazy talk.
Jo Jo Oh, really. What happened when we took that cruise to Europe?
Brenda "The Case of the Capsized Cruise Ship".
Darcy And that field trip to the mining town?
Brenda "The Mining Town Massacre".
Jo Jo Sheila's slumber party?
Brenda "The Slumber Blunder".
Darcy It's not you, Brenda. It just comes with the territory of being a teen detective, I guess.
Brenda I understand. I'll just go home and work on my Civil War re-enactment. You girls have fun.

Brenda exits

Darcy Now look what we've done. I promised I wouldn't let success go to my head and I've already forced my best friend off of the set. Brenda Bly!

Brenda appears from the wings

Brenda Yeah, Darcy?
Darcy What am I thinking? Of course you can stay.
Brenda Are you sure?
Darcy Heck, yeah. I was just being a silly.
Autumn Darcy, this is a closed rehearsal.
Darcy Doesn't the star have any pull in this company?
Autumn Fine, but if something happens, don't come crying to me.

Music No. 3b: Tension Underscore

Let's take it from Darcy's reprise. (*To Brenda, pointedly*) Anyone *not* going to the moon, kindly leave the stage.

The remaining members of the cast go into the wings

Brenda Thanks so much, Darcy, for letting me stay and watch. I promise nothing bad is going to happen.

Music No. 4: Next Stop the Moon: Reprise (*Darcy*)

Brenda exits

Darcy moves c and takes a pose. The spotlight comes on and shines on the backdrop

Autumn (*calling to the light booth at the back of the house*) Madeline, spotlight on the star.
Darcy Me! On me!

The spotlight quickly finds Darcy. As soon as it hits her, she smiles

(*Singing*)   On with my space suit
                          Off with a bang
                          I've packed my suitcase
                          Said goodbye to all the gang
                          An adventure of a lifetime
                          Is gonna happen soon
                          Buckle up ladies
                          Next stop — the ...

A strobe light flickers over Darcy. In slow motion, a sandbag on a rope is dropped from up above and lands directly on Darcy's head. She collapses to the stage. The music stops and the Lights return to normal

All the girls run on stage

Autumn Cut!
Jo Jo Darcy, are you OK?
Bridget She's out cold.

Van Strander enters, quickly followed by the uniformed school security guard, Cecil, who wears glasses and a cap at all times

Van Strander What in heaven's name is going on here?
Autumn Darcy's been knocked out cold.
Cecil (*trying to take charge*) All righty, rootie, girls. There's nothing to see here. Step back. Nothing to see here. Give the girl some room.

Van Strander pulls Cecil aside

Van Strander What did I tell you? I knew something bad would happen.
Cecil Now don't you worry there, Vera. Cecil's got it all under control. Stay with the girl. I'll go notify the authorities.
Van Strander No, don't you dare. What would the parents think? We can't blemish the school's impeccable reputation.
Cecil Ya sure, but just the same, you know, seems like serious business there, Vera.
Van Strander But aren't you a man of the law? We don't need pesky police nosing around. We've got you.
Cecil I am pretty quick on my feet.
Van Strander You certainly are.
Cecil And I have one of those Sherlock Holmes hats.
Van Strander Help me get her to the Nurse's Office.

Cecil and Van Strander attend to Darcy

Autumn What have I done? I've put my own star in mortal danger.
Bridget It's just awful. Who's going to get her part?
Autumn Bridget! A dear friend of ours was nearly killed. Priorities please! (*She moves to Darcy, sits her up and shakes her*) Darcy, can you hear me? I need you for costume fittings by six!
Van Strander Costume fittings my Aunt Maude. You certainly don't think this show is going on, do you?
Autumn But it's scheduled to open in two days.
Van Strander That's too bad.
Autumn I'll get you comps.
Van Strander I said no!

Brenda Miss Van Strander, have the police been notified?
Cecil Yes, well, we've decided to handle this eternally.
Van Strander Internally.
Cecil That too.
Brenda I assume you would like to keep this as low profile as possible.
Van Strander Well, yes. There's really no reason to panic anyone just yet.
Brenda But that's exactly what we'd be doing if we cancelled the show.
Van Strander Mmm. Little Miss Marbles has a point. Fine, for now the show is on. But one more mishap, and I am pulling this show over! Mr Sessille!

Cecil and Van Strander drag Darcy off stage

Autumn I can't tell you how grateful I am, Brenda Bly. You convinced Van Strander to keep the show on. You're a true friend. A true friend. (*She turns to go; to the other girls*) You see. She showed up, and look what happened.
Gidget It's like some sort of curse.
Autumn Remind me to tell box office, she's not allowed in on opening night.

All but Brenda exit

The Lights dim

Music No. 4a: Tension Underscore

Brenda is alone on stage. She gets out her flashlight and starts searching the stage area

Suddenly, Buddy jumps out from the wings

Buddy Boo!
Brenda Buddy! How did you get in here? Boys are strictly prohibited inside Whitney Ellis.
Buddy I climbed over the fence. It's gonna take more than a ten foot wall and barbed wire to keep this fella away from his gal.
Brenda You really shouldn't do things like that. It's too dangerous.
Buddy That's a risk I'm willing to take.
Brenda Buddy, don't be a hero.
Buddy Can't help it. It's in the blood. Come on, I just passed McFrosties and there's a hot fudge sundae with our name on it.
Brenda I can't. You'll never guess what happened.
Buddy You dreamt about me all night long, and vowed never to love another man as long as you live.

Brenda No, silly. Darcy was attacked.

Buddy You mean to say you don't dream about me.

Brenda Of course, I dream about you. More than a girl my age should.

Buddy You wanna know what I dream?

Brenda No. A girl shouldn't know about things like that. It's inappropriate.

Buddy Hey, I got an idea. Let's sneak out your father's Studebaker again.

Brenda That was reckless and you know it.

Buddy But tonight is our anniversary.

Brenda It is?

Buddy Six months to this very night, we shared our first soda at McFrosties.

Brenda Didn't we celebrate an anniversary last week?

Buddy Six months ago last week, we held hands for the very first time.

Brenda Goodness, let's not forget the first time we accidentally swapped our chewing gum.

Buddy That's tomorrow! You remembered! (*He hugs her*) Come on, let's go somewhere less academic.

Brenda Buddy, Darcy was just nearly killed. Didn't you wonder what all the commotion was just about?

Buddy I figured Van Strander finally lost her mind, and attacked a student.

Brenda Perhaps she did.

Buddy Oh no, you've got that look again.

Brenda What look?

Buddy That "I'm off to solve a case, and Buddy Rodgers doesn't exist" look.

Brenda Just let me get to the bottom of this, and I'm all yours. It shouldn't take too long.

Buddy That's what you said with "'The Case of the Cranky Clydesdale'".

Brenda That was a tricky one, wasn't it? But I figured it out eventually. Brenda Bly always gets her man.

Buddy Geez, for a teen detective, sometimes you're not very good at noticing the obvious.

Brenda What are you talking about?

Buddy There's a man standing right in front of you, Brenda Bly. And you're looking right through him.

Brenda Not another ghost.

Buddy I might as well be. Good luck on your case, Brenda Bly.

Buddy exits

Brenda (*making to chase after him*) Buddy! (*She stops herself*)

Music No. 5: I Always Get My Man (*Brenda*)

A villain waits out in the night
It's up to me to make it right

I get each man I keep in sight
But one

Be he jewel thief or con
Be it midnight or dawn
When the pressure's put upon
I always get my man
Supernat'ral or real
If they frighten or steal
I'll expose the slimy heel
And get my man

I'll inspect every clue
Check the phone records too
And the swindler gets his due
I always get my man
Watch me dusting for prints
List'ning in through the vents
I cash in my fear for sense
And get my man

There is not a crook who can outwit me
There is not a case I haven't cracked
But the one man I dream of kissing
Always winds up missing
Sad, but a fact

Through the rain, sleet or snow
I'll pursue any foe
Let the lawless bandit know
I always get my man
I will search low and high
For that dastardly guy
Or my name's not Brenda Bly
I get my man

No 5a: Scene Change Incidental

Brenda exits

SCENE 3

The Hospital

A sign is placed DL. *There are two arrows on it, pointing in opposite directions; one is marked "Maternity", the other "Morgue". A folding hospital screen is wheeled on* UR

The Lights come up. Autumn, Bridget, Gidget and Jo Jo pace around the waiting room

Van Strander enters

Van Strander Congratulations, ladies. After fifty years of the most spotless reputation in education, you've managed to plunge the Whitney Ellis Private School for Girls into the depths of utter embarrassment and despair.

Autumn Miss Van Strander, be straight with me. Darcy. How bad is she?

Van Strander I'm not going to lie, Autumn. It's pretty ugly.

Autumn But what about her performance as Rocket Girl?

Van Strander I was talking about her performance of Rocket Girl.

Bridget Miss Van Strander, it's the casting that's all wrong. I had my own television show, and now I'm playing an alien. It's an outrage!

Van Strander What do you expect, my dear? Life in the theatre is nothing but one disappointment after the other.

Gidget (*to Bridget*) You didn't have your own television show. I had my own television show, and you tagged along for the ride.

Bridget It was "The Bridget and Gidget Show", thank you very much. Bridget came first. You were just excess baggage.

Van Strander Enough! I have heard enough out of all of you.

Bridget But I can tap dance.

Gidget My dead pony tap dances better than you!

Bridget It was our pony and you killed it!

Van Strander What part of "enough" do you not understand? Now out of my way. Darcy is going to be fine. Hospital smells make me nauseous. So someone please explain to me why I'm standing here talking to yard apes in poodle skirts?

Autumn You're absolutely right, Miss Van Strander. The twins, they're all wrong. But if you'll just give me a chance ...

Bridget Need I remind you that we have had correspondence with Vincent Minnelli?

Autumn In the form of a restraining order!

Van Strander You see, ladies. Look around you. Overblown egos. Back-stabbing. Deceit. Welcome to the theatre.

Van Strander exits. Bridget and Gidget follow her off

Autumn This is all my fault. I knew I should have played the part myself.

Jo Jo puts her hand on Autumn's shoulder, as if to comfort her

Jo Jo Autumn, don't be ridiculous. You would have been awful as the lead.

Dr Sniffles enters with some hospital charts

Dr Sniffles Anyone here know a girl named Darcy?
Autumn Darcy Warner. Yes.
Jo Jo How is she?
Dr Sniffles She's dead.
Autumn What!
Dr Sniffles Oops. Wrong chart. I hate it when that happens. (*He looks at another chart*) Darcy Warner. She's fine. You can see her now.

Nurse Ivy rolls Darcy on in a wheelchair. She wears a matching pink pyjama set with fluffy pink slippers. She has a large bandage round her head

Brenda runs in

Brenda (*to Dr Sniffles*) Excuse me; I'm looking for Darcy Warner.
Dr Sniffles Never heard of her.

Dr Sniffles exits

Brenda (*seeing Darcy and running over to her*) Darcy, I'm so sorry. I feel just horrible.
Darcy Do I know you?
Brenda Of course you do, silly. I'm your best friend. Brenda Bly.
Darcy Brenda Bly?
Brenda That's right. Teen detective.
Darcy I don't remember.
Brenda Oh no. I've given my best friend amnesia.
Jo Jo Come on, Brenda. You didn't give her amnesia. Whoever dropped that sandbag on her head gave her amnesia.
Brenda That's right. And now it's up to me to figure out who it was.
Autumn But what about "Rocket Girl"? It opens in two days, and my leading lady has lost her mind.
Darcy I was the lead? How was I?

Jo Jo You were all right. A bit over the top.

Darcy I can't believe it. This is just my luck. I finally get the lead and I can't remember it.

Brenda I swear I'm going to catch the person who did this.

Darcy Why would someone do this to me? Was I annoying?

Girls Of course not.

Darcy Was I rude?

Girls Don't be silly.

Darcy Was I a bad actress?

They are all silent, not sure what to say

Brenda I have to go. I've got a case to solve. I'll let you know what I find out.

Darcy Thanks...

Brenda Brenda Bly.

Darcy Brenda Bly. Teen Detective.

Brenda That's right.

Brenda and Jo Jo exit. Dr Sniffles enters

Dr Sniffles Now let's see how our patient is doing? How are you, sweetie?

Darcy I don't know who I am.

Dr Sniffles That's OK. I didn't know who I was 'til *way* past college. (*He puts his stethoscope in his ears and checks Darcy's heartbeat. He writes something on a pad, and then stands up. He beckons Autumn over to him*)

Autumn Yes?

Dr Sniffles (*still with the stethoscope in his ears, so shouting very loudly*) I didn't want to worry your friend, but it doesn't look good. Not good at all. (*He moves* US *to study his charts*)

Nurse Wilder and Nurse Iris enter US *and join Dr Sniffles*

Autumn Pay him no mind, Darcy. I'm sure you'll be fine. You just need to be reminded of certain things. I'll take you back to the theatre. Maybe being in familiar surroundings will jog your memory.

Darcy You're very kind. All my friends seem very nice.

Autumn Oh, the nicest. You're very well liked.

Darcy Nurse, can I see a mirror?

Nurse Ivy magically produces a mirror and hands it to Darcy

Music No. 6: A Girl Like Me (*Darcy, Autumn, Dr Sniffles, Nurse Ivy, Nurse Wilder and Nurse Iris*)

Oh, look at that complexion. Like a porcelain doll! I'm adorable!
(*Singing*) I had it all
First thing this morning
Then came the fall
Without a warning
Who-oo-oo
Could hurt a girl like me?

	Am I not sweet?
Autumn	As candy
Darcy	Am I not charming?
Autumn	And then some
Darcy	Pure and elite
Autumn	Like Doris Day
Darcy	What's so alarming
	Who-oo-oo
	Could hurt a girl like me?

Dr Sniffles wheels Darcy around the stage; the others dance

	I've done my best
Ensemble	You've done your best
Darcy	I've done my duty
Ensemble	You've done your duty
Darcy	Unlike the rest
Ensemble	Unlike the rest
Darcy	I live for beauty
Ensemble	Woah-oh-oh-oh-oh-oh-oh
	Oh-oh-oh-oh-oh-oh
	Oh-oh-oh-oh-oh-oh

| **Nurses** ⎫
Autumn ⎬
Dr Sniffles ⎭ | One of the most
Lovely of faces
Always the toast
You are what grace is
Who
Could hurt a girl like
Who
Could hurt a girl like… | **Darcy** Don't like to boast
No need for braces
From coast to coast
I am what grace is
Who
Could hurt a girl like
Who
Could hurt a girl like… |

Dr Sniffles produces a large syringe, which he plunges into Darcy's arm

Darcy (*speaking*) ME! (*She passes out*)

Music No. 6a: Scene Change Incidental

Everyone exits

SCENE 4

Backstage

A costume rack or two, the rocket ship flat (turned to face US*) and a few flats are brought on stage. The* US *curtains are edged in slightly*

The Lights are very dim

Buddy runs on to the darkened stage dressed in black, and wearing a ski mask. He rolls across the floor and manoeuvres through the darkness, as if he were a spy on a secret mission. He is followed by Stu, hobbling on one foot, also wearing a ski mask

Buddy Come on. We're almost there.
Stu I can't see a thing, Buddy! I've gone blind! We break into an all-girl's school and as soon as I'm over the wall, I'm blind! My mother told me this would happen.
Buddy You're not blind. You've got your mask on backwards.

Stu takes off his mask. It is apparent that currently he is in the middle of his worst nightmare

Stu I can't go any further, Buddy. My foot's killing me.
Buddy Just relax. We made it over the wall. No-one saw us.
Stu I think I cut my foot climbing over the fence. It cut right through the shoe.
Buddy You'll be fine.
Stu Do you want to be expelled from Lorber Academy? Do you? Because that's what's going to happen when they catch us.
Buddy No-one's going to catch us.
Stu I don't understand what we're doing here anyway.
Buddy Brenda has fallen in love with someone else, and I'm going to find out who it is with my very own eyes.
Stu How?
Buddy Girls talk, Stu. I realize that, never having any contact whatsoever with a girl, this news might come as a shock to you.
Stu The only female I know is my mother, and she scares the daylights out of me.

Buddy Well, I'm not afraid of women, and I'm going to get to the bottom of this. Now let's go.

Stu I don't know if I can. I hurt my foot real bad.

Buddy You're a total basket case. Why did I let you come with me anyway?

Stu You didn't let me come. You made me come. I begged you to not make me come.

Buddy Well, I have a good mind to send you back.

Stu Please, send me back. I want to go back.

Buddy You're not going anywhere. Let me see your foot. (*He pulls off Stu's shoe*)

Stu Be careful with my foot. I've only got one more.

Buddy Don't look.

Stu Is it bleeding?

There is a sound from the wings

Van Strander (*off*) I'll check in here.

Buddy Oh, no. It's that Van Strander. We've got to hide.

Buddy and Stu hide, Buddy dropping Stu's shoe in the process

Van Strander enters in a fury. She storms in and searches backstage

Van Strander No use hiding, you good-for-nothing brutes. I'll find you. I may not be able to see you, but I can smell you. (*She sniffs around the room like a bloodhound*)

After a moment, Cecil enters carrying a bottle of wine behind his back

Cecil taps Van Strander on the shoulder. She immediately spins around and slaps him across the face

Van Strander Cecil! What did I tell you about sneaking up on me? You know I'm high strung.

Cecil I'm sorry, sweetie. I wanted to surprise you. (*He presents her with the bottle of wine*)

Van Strander Apple wine? I have a Defcon Five crisis going on, and you're playing "Find the cheap wine"?

Cecil I thought we could have a little Cecil/Vera time. I could bring the Perry Como records. You could unwind a bit.

Van Strander Cecil, I can't think about that right now. Something more troubling is brewing.

Cecil You're cooking chowder?

Van Strander No, you imbecile. I saw two hoodlums crawling over the
  fence.
Cecil No!
Van Strander Yes!

Cecil and Van Strander simultaneously look down and see Stu's shoe

> Did I not tell you! There's a man on the premises and they've already
> started taking off their clothes.

Cecil I wouldn't worry about it, Vera. Probably one of the girl's boyfriends
  sneaking in for a little attention. I think it's sweet.
Van Strander You think it's sweet, do you? (*She sidles up to him and
  seductively runs her fingers over his chest*) Hot blooded testosterone
  jockeys, disobeying the rules, and putting my girls in harm's way.
Cecil Everybody needs a little lovin' now and then.
Van Strander You want some lovin', Cecil? You find me those boys who
  crawled over these walls.
Cecil And if I do?
Van Strander I'll give you a surprise that'll make your chest hairs stand on
  end.
Cecil Can do!
Van Strander And if you don't find them, you can take your Perry Como
  records and go home. Alone.
Cecil Couldn't we just ——
Van Strander Cecil, that was not a request!

Music No. 7: Find Me That Man (*Van Strander and Cecil*)

Do you realize the gravity of this situation? There has been a penetration
of the male form into my "Girls Only"!
> (*Singing*) Find me that man
>> Who's hiding in the shadows
>> So I can string him
>> Bring him
>> Like any man
>> I'm certain when I find him
>> How easily I will grind him
>>
>> By nature a man is vicious
>> So true
>> He's slippery and malicious
>> That too
>> Still won't he taste delicious
>> In stew
>> Find me that man
>> Or you're in hot water too

	Find me that man
	Can't you
	Find me that man
	Won't you
	Find me that man darling do
Cecil	I'll find that man and in no time when we got him
	We're gonna get down to the bottom
	Search high and low so that aggravating devil
	Is on the level
	True — this stranger could be seedy
	You can bet that I'll be speedy
	Do I got it — yes indeedy
	Babe you can count on Cecil
	Find me that man
	I will
	Find me that man
	Yes, I'll
	Find me that man darling do
Van Strander ⎫	Three's a crowd
Cecil ⎭	So let's go catch that creep
	Then at last we'll be alone
	Such a fright, I'm certain I won't sleep
Van Strander	You'll protect me, dear
Cecil	If anyone can clear a weasel
	Vera, you can count on Cecil

V.S. Find me that man
Who's slipping through our
fingers
Once I've attacked him
Sacked him
I'll thank the man
Who found him on the double
I'll make it worth his trouble
You're ready for some
romancing
Do tell
For drinking and maybe dancing
Sounds swell
You want to see me prancing
Ah well
Find me that man
Or there's not one chance in hell

Cecil I'll find that man and in
no time when we got him
We're gonna get down
to the bottom
Search high and low so that
aggravating devil
is on the level
True — this stranger could be
seedy
You can bet that I'll be speedy
Do I got it — yes indeedy
Babe you can count on Cecil

Cecil	Find me that man
Van Strander	Let's go
	Find me that man
	Let's go
	Find me that man darling do

Find me that man
Let's go
Find me that man
Let's go
Find me that man darling do

One more time!

Find me that man
Let's go
Find me that man
Let's go
Find me that man darling
Do!

Music No. 7a: Playoff/Scene change

Van Strander and Cecil exit

SCENE 5

On stage

The spaceship flat is moved to face DS and the flats and costume racks are removed

The Lights come up. The girls — Candy, Madeline, Bridget, Gidget, Jo Jo, Darcy and Brenda among them — are preparing for rehearsal

Autumn enters carrying a large can of red paint and a brush

Autumn OK ladies, I realize we have had some bumps on the path to my greatness, but that is not reason to give up the ghost. We've got a show to put on. Sets do not build themselves. Jo Jo, paint those craters. Candy?

Candy runs over with excitement

I realize you only have one line in the show, but I'm afraid it's been cut. (*She walks away from Candy, crossing over to Madeline*)

Candy is left, as always, speechless

Bridget (*to Autumn*) You mean the show's going on. Who's going to play Rocket Girl?
Autumn Darcy, of course.

Brenda runs up to Darcy

Brenda Darcy, you got your memory back?
Darcy Have we met?
Gidget Autumn, who are you kidding? This show is doomed.
Autumn Don't say that!
JoJo She has a point. We have a better chance at flying to the moon ourselves than getting this thing off the ground.
Autumn All great works of art comes with a little heartache. Do you think greatness comes easy, ladies?
Darcy But it just seems impossible. I don't even remember what a moon looks like.
Autumn The moon. What *the* moon looks like.
Darcy See?
Autumn I do see, Darcy. I see Possibility in the face of Adversity. And that's what makes it all so exciting.

Music No. 8: Showbiz (*Autumn and "Rocket Girl" cast*)

> (*Singing*) You've a leading role
> That could make a star
> Then a sandbag falls
> And you're less than par
> You don't have a clue
> As to who you are
> You know what that is —
> Showbiz!
> (*Crossing to Candy*)
> If your only line
> Has a tragic plight
> And you play a mute
> On your op'ning night
> So your claim to fame
> Is fifth to the right

You know what that is ——

Candy makes as if to sing, but Autumn covers her mouth

	Showbiz!

Showbiz!
So we'll keep on chugging on
Till that great day we're redeemed
We'll keep chugging, yes we will
Till we're the cream of the crop
Jo Jo   Or just creamed
Autumn (*crossing to Madeline*) You've come all this way
From a place called France
And you stomp around
In a zombie trance
You may can-can-can
But you can't-can't dance
You know what that is ——
Madeline   *Showbiz!*
All   Yes we'll keep on chugging on
And we won't give up the ghost
We'll keep chugging, yes we will
Autumn   Till we're the toast of the town
Bridget |
Gidget | Or just toast
All   On and on up that hill we'll go
We won't settle for status quo
In this business that they call show
Till we're the top of the heap
We're in knee deep
Autumn (*crossing to Bridget and Gidget*) You were once a star
You had found your place
Then you lost it all
And to your disgrace
You can't win the lead
In a three-legged race
You know what that is
Bridget   I know what that is all right. That's bullsh'...
Autumn   Showbiz!
All   So we're days away
From our big première
And our stomachs turn
Cause we're filled with fear
Be it do or die

> We will persevere
> Through the drama that is
> Showbiz! Showbiz! Showbiz! Showbiz!

Autumn (*speaking*) Now that's more like it. We're not about to take a back seat to defeat. Jo Jo, get these sets out of here. (*Picking up the pot of paint and a brush*) Madeline, take this paint and touch up the rocket.
Madeline Bonjour!
Autumn Paint. Paint? Monet?
Madeline Bonjour!
Autumn Come on, this isn't rocket science. Look at the pretty paint brush. See? You dip it in the can. See? Dip? Dip?

Jo Jo and Brenda move the rocket ship flat

Van Strander is revealed standing behind the flat, staring at Autumn with her arms crossed

Doesn't take an idiot, Frenchy. Dip, dip and slap it on the tired old hunk of metal.

Autumn, intending to paint the rocket ship, slaps the paintbrush across Van Strander's face, getting paint in Van Strander's eyes. Van Strander doesn't budge. She is so mad, she can't even speak. As if that's not bad enough ...

See? Any idiot can do this. Dip, dip and slap. (*She does it again*) Dip, dip. Sl ... (*She realizes what she has done*)

Music No. 8a: Showbiz: Reprise and Scene Change

	(*Singing*) You have bared your soul
	For your favourite art
	You have formed the words
	That express your heart
	With one fatal stroke
	You'll be ripped apart
Girls	You know what that is
Autumn	Ah, put a sock in it.

The US *curtains close and the Lights go down on the* US *area*

SCENE 6

The Prop Room

To the R *of the stage, a costume shop, as represented by a costume rack, a costumed mannequin, bolts of fabric, etc. is set up, possibly trucked on. To the* L *a prop shop, represented by a large trunk and various theatrical props, is set up or trucked on simultaneously*

The Lights come up on the prop room

Music No. 8b: Prop Room Underscore

Brenda enters carrying a large sword. Jo Jo follows her in

Jo Jo Did you see that, Brenda? Van Strander got it right in the eyes. Score!
Brenda Something else caught my eye. Look what I found backstage. (*She produces the sword*)
Jo Jo What the heck is that?
Brenda Two guesses.
Jo Jo The sword used to cut the rope of the sandbag?
Brenda Exactly. I think our culprit ran to the prop shop and grabbed the first thing that could cut that rope.
Jo Jo And now you've decided to check out the prop shop — at night — alone. You will never learn, will you?
Brenda Don't worry. What could possibly happen to us? (*She opens the trunk*)

Buddy stands up from inside the box and screams

Brenda and Jo Jo scream back

Buddy! You nearly scared the daylights out of me.
Buddy You didn't do wonders for me either.
Brenda I haven't had such a fright since we were nearly locked in King Kaaman's tomb for the rest of eternity.
Buddy I've heard all about "The Case of the Crummy Mummy". Spare me.
Brenda What are you doing here?
Buddy No. I think the question is what are you doing here?
Brenda I go to school here.
Buddy Oh, right. Well, I think the real question is what is Stu doing here?

Buddy drags Stu out from behind a curtain

Stu Why do you have to get me involved?
Jo Jo A stowaway. Now that's more like it.
Buddy Stu. You remember Jo Jo.
Stu You know I can't talk to girls.
Buddy Just say hallo. She won't bite.
Jo Jo But I might nibble. (*She smiles flirtatiously at Stu*)

Jo Jo chases Stu off stage

Brenda Do you have any idea how much trouble I will get into if Miss Van
Strander catches you here?
Buddy Who is he?
Brenda Who is who?
Buddy This other fella. What's his name?
Brenda There is no other fella, Buddy. Gosh, don't you know by now how
much I care about you? You're my guy.
Buddy I just miss you so much sometimes.
Brenda And I miss you. But just because I'm busy doesn't mean I don't
think you're the cat's meow.
Buddy It wouldn't hurt for you to tell me now and again.
Brenda Hey, Buddy Rogers?
Buddy Yeah, Brenda Bly?
Brenda I think you're swell.
Buddy I think you're pretty neato yourself.
Brenda And as soon as I solve this case, I'm going to show you just how
swell I think you are. But for now, I have to think about Darcy. Please,
she's my best friend.
Buddy And what am I, huh? Just what am I?
Brenda Why, you're my best guy. You're my own Buddy Rogers. And I'm
just crazy about you.
Buddy You certainly have a funny way of showing it.
Brenda You want me to show you how much I care about you? Once I figure
out who attacked Darcy, we'll sneak out my father's Studebaker again.
Buddy You're just saying that.
Brenda No, I mean it. And you can go wherever you want. As fast as you
want. As far as you want.
Buddy As far as I want?
Brenda We'll go back to the place where we first kissed. Remember? On
the dance floor?
Buddy Remember? Next Tuesday it'll be four months, two weeks, and six
days.
Brenda You and me, dancing the night away at the VFW Hall.
Buddy They thought we were college students.

Brenda The soft lights. The paper streamers. The music.

Music No. 9: Cha Cha Cha (*Buddy and Brenda*)

Buddy It was magic, Brenda. Pure magic.
Brenda (*singing*) You and me
                      And the cha cha cha
                      To the beat
                      Of the cha cha cha
Buddy   By the sea
                      Hearing cha cha cha
                      Feel the heat
                      Of the cha cha cha
Brenda   Oh Buddy how the whole world was spinning
Buddy   Brenda it was just the beginning
                      Crowds were watching us twirl
                      Me and my girl
Brenda   Watching us fly
                      Me and my guy
Brenda | Doing the cha cha cha
Buddy | Doing the cha cha cha
Brenda   Driving home
Buddy   To the cha cha cha
Brenda   Feels so good
Buddy   It's the cha cha cha
Brenda   Feel the chrome
Buddy   Hear that cha cha cha
Brenda   On the hood
                      Thanks to cha cha cha
Buddy   Oh Brenda
                      Could you feel my love growing
Brenda   Buddy how your fondness was showing
Buddy   You and me there on top
Brenda   Also that cop
Buddy   Temperatures drop
Brenda   Making us stop
Brenda | Doing the cha cha cha
Buddy | Doing the cha cha cha

Dance break

The Lights change. The stage fills with dry ice, a mirrorball flies in

   *Ballroom dancing couples enter and join Brenda and Buddy in a fantasy
   sequence recalling their first dance*

Brenda ⎤	We'll be fine
Buddy ⎟	With our cha cha cha
Backing ⎟	Through the years
vocals (*off*) ⎦	We will cha cha cha
	You'll be mine
	And we'll cha cha cha
	Have no fears
	We've got the cha cha cha
Brenda	Oh Buddy, now our life is before us
Buddy	Brenda
	How our kids will implore us
	To hear it again
Brenda	'bout way back when

The dancing couples exit

The mirrorball flies out; the setting returns to the prop room

Buddy	Memories of
Brenda	Falling in love
Buddy ⎤	Doing the cha cha cha (AH!)
Brenda ⎦	Doing the cha cha cha (AH!)
	Doing the cha cha cha (AH!)
	Doing the cha cha cha (AH!)
	Cha cha cha cha cha
All	Cha cha cha!

Buddy and Brenda start to kiss. There is a sound off stage

Brenda It's Miss Van Strander. Quick. Hide.

Buddy hides

Van Strander slowly enters. She is feeling her way around. She wears dark glasses, and red paint covers her face

Van Strander Who's there?

Brenda It's me, Brenda Bly. How are your eyes?

Van Strander I can't see a single thing, the paint is cracking my eyelashes, and I've never felt such mind-numbing pain in all of my life.

Brenda But aren't your glasses cute?

Van Strander School hours are over. Get to your room now. Unless you want to be written up.

Brenda No, I'll leave. You know how I'm a stickler for the rules.

Van Strander Yeah, so you are. Now get out.
Brenda I'll see you tomorrow.

Brenda exits

Van Strander listens to hear Brenda leave. Buddy comes out of hiding and tries to sneak behind Van Strander. He gets almost to the exit

Van Strander (*calling out*) And where do you think you're going?

Buddy freezes

Yes, I'm talking to you. You think I don't know you're there? I may not be able to see very well, but I've got a sniffer like a bloodhound.
Buddy Listen, I can ——
Van Strander Shh. Let's make sure she's gone. (*She sniffs around*) I think we're alone. (*Suddenly, she throws herself at Buddy, wrapping her arms around him from behind*) Darling, will you forgive me for snapping at you earlier?
Buddy Huh?
Van Strander Oh, don't play games with me, Cecil. I know that scent anywhere. Tiger Musk. I bought that especially for my own little tiger. (*She growls*)

Buddy stands frozen and terrified

You are my little tiger, aren't you, Cecil? Aren't you?

Buddy (*trying a desperate impersonation of Cecil*) Yah, sure.

The Lights snap to the Costume Shop on the other side of the stage

Music No. 9a: Scene change incidental

SCENE 7

The Costume Shop

Music No. 10: I Always Get My Man: Reprise (*Jo Jo*)

Stu runs in and hides behind some costumes on a rail. Jo Jo enters directly after him

Jo Jo Oh, come on. Don't be such a 'fraidy cat. I just want to talk. You can't hide forever.

       (*Singing*) Be he hero or wimp
            Be he genius or simp
            Be he Tarzan or a chimp
            I never get my man
            Rich or poor — I don't care
            Awful bore — debonair
            Still I think it's only fair
            I get my man

Jo Jo pulls apart costumes on a rack. Stu stands there shaking in fear

Music No. 11: Jo Jo's Undercover (*Jo Jo*)

Jo Jo Oh, come on. Why are you so afraid? I'm just a girl.
Stu Yeah, well, I'm not really that ...
Jo Jo Interested?
Stu Familiar. I don't know any girls, really.
Jo Jo Well, I think it's about time you did. Cards on the table. What do you want to know?
Stu If I can leave.
Jo Jo You're just gonna leave me here? Who's going to protect me?
Stu It's not you that needs protecting.

Jo Jo (*singing*)	But can't you see this damsel in distress
	I'm awf'ly frightened now I must confess
	I need a man who's strong and musclebound
Stu	I'll go out and see if that man can't be found
Jo Jo	Let's go undercover baby
	Let's go down below
	Once we're undercover baby
	Discover a clue you really ought to know

Cecil (*off*) Anybody in there?
Jo Jo It's Cecil. Quick, hide!

Jo Jo pushes Stu into the costume rack

   Cecil enters

Cecil What's going on in here?
Jo Jo Nothing.
Cecil Who were you talking to?

Jo Jo No-one.

Cecil I heard voices.

Jo Jo That's really between you and your therapist.

Cecil I heard a male voice. In this room.

Jo Jo You can't just barge in here and accuse me without a warrant. This is harassment in the first degree.

Cecil This isn't your home, Sass McFrass! This is a costume shop on the grounds of a school that I am paid marginally to protect. And it is my job to see to it that all shenanigans cease and assist. (*He thinks for a moment, confused*) Seize and in̲sist? Cease and ... Well, no matter. I have every right to search this room, and that's exactly what I'm going to do. Now out!

Jo Jo But ——

Cecil It's a criminal offence to interfere with official police business.

Jo Jo You got your security licence in the mail!

Cecil I said out.

Cecil pushes Jo Jo out of the room

(*Making his way to the costume rack*) Now it's just us fellas in the room. Far be it from me to get violent in front of a lady. (*He reaches for the costume rack*) Come out, you ruffian. Fight like a man. (*He pulls aside the costume rack*)

Stu is now dressed up like a French woman, with wig, beret, slinky dress and heels. Stu looks terrified and stares at Cecil for a moment

Stu (*in a high-pitched voice*) Bonjour!

The Lights snap back to the prop room

SCENE 8

The Prop Room

Music No. 12: I Always Get My Man: Reprise (*Van Strander*)

Buddy is pinned against the wall. Van Strander is whispering in his ear

Van Strander You will forgive me my sweet, won't you? My poor, sweet Cecil was starving for attention, and I turned on him like bad cheese.

Buddy Obviously you can't see at all.

Van Strander Just blurry forms ... But I don't need eyes to see how I've been neglecting you.

Brenda enters during the song, unseen by Van Strander and Buddy

> (*Singing*) So I'm blind as bat
> Pay no mind to all that
> 'cause I'm purring like a cat (Prrrr!)
> I'm gonna get my man
> I will grope my way through
> Let my hands form a coup
> Grab a hold of what is due
> And get my man

Van Strander gives Buddy a big kiss

There's more where that came from. I'll meet you in five minutes in my office. 'Til then, Tiger.

Van Strander walks past Brenda, who is in complete shock, and exits

Brenda immediately approaches Buddy

Brenda Of all the two-timing, dishonest, degenerate scum I've come across in my day, I've never seen anything so repulsive in my life.
Buddy That? No, she thought I was ——
Brenda All this time, I thought you came here to see me. And you came to see her. Vera Van Strander. My headmistress. Where does the madness end?
Buddy I did come here to see you!
Brenda Spare me the excuses, Tiger. You forget I'm Brenda Bly, Teen Detective. You're not about to pull a fast one over me.
Buddy If you would get your head out of this case for one second, you would realize how absolutely ridiculous you're being.
Brenda I happen to be very good at what I do.
Buddy You're good at solving cases, but when it comes to relationships, I'm afraid you've followed this trail to a dead end.
Brenda Boy did I ever!
Buddy What are you waiting for? Go solve your case. It's obviously more important than I am.
Brenda I will go solve it. As for you and I, case closed.

Brenda runs out

Buddy watches her go

Music No. 13: A Thief in the Night (*Buddy and Brenda*)

Buddy   Once I was safe
                             That's the way it has always been
                             Open your heart
                             And you can't lock it back again
                             One starry night
                             My reality splintered

The US *curtains slowly open and the costume shop is removed or trucked
off* R. *A black camera strap is set on the floor* US

   Brenda enters UR *with a flashlight*

Dim lights come up on the UR *area to suggest the darkened theatre*

                             And she entered
                             As I let her in
Brenda   Gone in a flash
                             Left here wounded and incomplete
                             Standing alone
                             With my world crumbled at my feet
                             He walked away
                             Leaving no trace — please find him
                             A criminal's walking the street
Buddy ⎤   Whoa-oh-oh-oh
Brenda ⎦   Someone has broken in
                             Stolen my heart
                             Like a thief in the night
                             Whoa-oh-oh-oh
                             Someone has broken in
                             Stolen my heart
                             Like a thief in the night

                             Maybe in time
                             The scene of the crime
                             Won't look like a bloody spree
                             And I'll start to feel
                             The wounds start to heal
                             But not as long as (she) he is running free

                             Call the police
                             Make a note of these awful deeds
                             Shout from the hills

'Til the whole village intercedes
Summon the force
Use the facts to compel them
And tell them
How your poor heart bleeds

Follow each lead
Chase him (her) down
Set off all alarms
Show no remorse
Let him (her) pay for the one he (she) harms
Fight 'til the day
We at last apprehend her (him)
And send her (him)
Back into my arms

Whoa-oh-oh-oh
Someone has broken in
Stolen my heart
Like a thief in the night
Whoa-oh-oh-oh
Someone has broken in
Stolen my heart
Like a thief in the night

Buddy exits

Brenda continues searching the stage for clues. Suddenly, her flashlight beam lands on the black camera strap

Brenda What's this? It looks like the strap to Darcy's camera. But where's the camera, that's what I want to know.

There is the clunk of a power switch being turned off and the Lights black out

(*Shining her flashlight around*) Hallo? Is anyone there? Buddy? (*She turns to look off stage*)

A sandbag falls from the rafters. Brenda screams, drops her flashlight and falls to the floor

A figure in black runs across the stage

The music builds. The Lights come up on Brenda's body lying C *with the sandbag by her side*

CURTAIN

ACT II

Music No. 14: Entr'acte and Opening Act II
(*The Company except Brenda*)

SCENE 1

On stage/backstage

The front curtains open. The lighting is dim. Brenda lies, as yet unseen, UC
*as she was at the end of Act I. The rest of the cast is on stage, dressed as
detectives. They carry flashlights and sneak about the stage as if they were
Brenda Bly*

Company (*singing*) More danger in the air
                Surrounds our favourite friend
                Just who, what, when and where
                Would want her life to end
                With broken heart she cried out bloody murder
                Now let's get back and see if someone heard her
                She won't die that's our objective
                Brenda Bly
                Teen detective

The company exits to reveal Brenda lying UC

Music No. 14a: Prop Room Underscore

*After a moment, Autumn enters carrying a flashlight. She is followed by
Jo Jo and Darcy, who cower behind her*

Jo Jo What exactly are we doing here?
Autumn I told you. I heard someone scream.
Jo Jo I don't know where you come from, but in my world, when someone
screams, you go the other way.
Autumn But someone could be in trouble.
Jo Jo Exactly. Us.

Madeline enters, walks up behind the others and stands, unknown to them, way too close

Madeline Bonjour!

Everyone nearly jumps out of her skin

Jo Jo Would you stop doing that? I'm gonna have to put a cow bell around your neck!
Autumn Jo Jo, don't yell at her.
Jo Jo She doesn't understand a word I'm saying.
Autumn She can see it in your expression.
Jo Jo Fine. (*She puts on a big smile and lightens up her face as if she were talking to a child*) You are driving me to drink, Frenchy. I don't know who dropped that sandbag on Darcy's head, but when we find out who it is, I'm going to ask them to drop one on you.

Madeline stares at Jo Jo without a clue, smiling back

Madeline (*after a beat*) Bonjour!
Jo Jo Look! Jerry Lewis. (*She points off stage*)

Madeline stares at Jo Jo without a clue, smiling back

Jerry Lewis! Er — croissant!
Madeline Mmm! Croissant!

Madeline licks her lips and runs off stage

Autumn sees Brenda lying on the stage with the sandbag next to her

Autumn Brenda Bly! Oh, no. They got Brenda Bly!

They all rush to Brenda

Brenda *Au contraire!* (*She jumps up quickly*) When being attacked, the best thing to do is lie motionless and act like you're down for the count.
Darcy You could have been killed.
Brenda I think that's exactly what they were hoping for.
Autumn But why would someone want you dead?
Brenda Why else?

Jo Jo You know too much?
Brenda Not yet. But I plan to. I'm going to solve this case if it's the last thing
  I do. And I think this holds the answer. (*She holds up the camera strap*)
Jo Jo What is it?
Brenda I found it backstage. I think it's the key to this puzzle. I just don't
  know how it fits. But I will. Believe me, I will. Or my name isn't ——
Voices (*off*)   Brenda Bly
                 Teen Detective.

Black-out

SCENE 2

McFrostie's Soda Shop

Music No. 14b: Soda Shop Incidental

*There is a soda shop counter UC, behind the line of the US curtains, and a small
table and two chairs DR; there is also a juke box. A sign saying "McFrostie's"
is flown in or brought on*

*The Lights come up. Wally, a middle-aged man with thick glasses and pants
far too short for him, is behind the counter, serving sodas to Bridget and
Gidget. Other schoolgirls are crowded round the juke box. Stu sits alone at
a table in a state of shock*

Buddy enters and heads for the soda counter

Bridget and Gidget stop Buddy

Bridget Hi, Buddy.
Buddy Gidget.
Gidget I'm Gidget. She's Bridget. There's quite an easy way to tell us apart,
  you know.
Bridget I'm the pretty one, and she's the one who looks like fish bait.
Gidget Skank!
Bridget Hag!
Gidget Overbite!
Bridget Underdeveloped calves!
Buddy Do you mind, girls? I didn't come here to chitchat. I've come here
  to drown my sorrows. (*He sits at the counter*) Hey, Wally, give me a cherry
  soda straight up with a milkshake chaser.
Wally I'm gonna need to see some ID.

Buddy looks at Wally, confused

No-one gets my sense of humour. I knew I shouldn't have gone to clown camp.

Buddy sees Stu and crosses to him

Buddy What happened to you last night?
Stu Buddy, I've seen the most horrible things. The security guard mistook me for that foreign exchange student.
Buddy You think that's bad. Van Strander thought I was her boyfriend!
Stu He tried to undo my bra.
Buddy Stu, you didn't.
Stu Of course not. I may be a guy, but as a girl I do have my standards. (*He crosses his legs*)

Jo Jo enters and runs over to Stu

Jo Jo Oh, thank God. Stu, I was so worried about you.
Stu Yeah, I could tell. You left me with that creep.
Jo Jo Hey, I came back, but when I looked in the costume shop you were gone. And Cecil was slow dancing with some girl.

Buddy looks at Stu

Stu One dance.
Jo Jo Some hag.
Stu Hag?
Wally Does she have a sister?
All Wally!

Darcy and Autumn enter

Autumn Well, well, well. If it isn't the heartbreaker himself.
Buddy Hey, I didn't break her heart. She broke mine.
Gidget What's this? You and Brenda broke up!
Bridget Out of my way, zit head!
Wally Buddy, no! Tell me it isn't so.
Buddy It's so, all right.
Stu Did you hear that, Jo Jo? Buddy's single.
Jo Jo No thanks. (*She wraps herself around Stu*) I already got a fella.
Stu But look at him. He's gorgeous.
Jo Jo Isn't that sweet? You're jealous.

Wally For godsakes, you've got to listen to me. If you've found someone who can stomach you, hang on to her with all your might. Another girl may never come along.

Buddy You've got to be kidding me? This is Buddy Rogers you're talking to.

Music No. 15: All-American Boy (*Buddy, Wally, Stu and girls*)

I was about due for an upgrade anyway. Brenda Bly! What does she know? Mark my words, when it gets out that I'm a free agent, there's gonna be lines around the block of girls just hoping to get a date with Buddy Rogers. I'm what makes this country so great. Why, I'm a National Treasure.

Jo Jo And so modest.

Buddy (*singing*) I don't mean to brag
                    But any fool can see
                    You
                    Would be proud too
                    If you were cool as me
                    Have you ever seen a fella look so good
                    I would date myself if I only could

                    So come on
                    Fall in line and join the parade
                    So come on
                    I'm the reason back seats were made
                    Everybody's rocking to the all-American boy

Girls }   Shoo-be-doo-be-wop
Stu   }   Shoo-be-doo-be-wop-wop
Wally }   Shoo-be-doo-be-wop
                    Shoo-be-doo-be-wop-wop

Buddy   I'm as cool as Como
                    Hot as apple pie
                    Watch 'em throw confetti
                    As I'm passing by
                    Such a sweet demeanour
                    And that perfect grin
                    What a crying shame I wasn't born a twin
                    So come on
                    Every muscle perfectly toned
                    So come on
                    Praise the Lord perfection's been loaned
                    Everybody's rocking to the all-American boy

Girls ⎤	Shoo-be-doo-be-wop
Stu ⎬	Shoo-be-doo-be-wop-wop
Wally ⎦	Shoo-be-doo-be-wop
	Shoo-be-doo-be-wop-wop
Buddy	Oh, say can you see a more stupendous sight
	What so gallantly I share
	Oh say can you see the future's looking bright
	With waves of amber hair
Company	Waves of amber hair
	Waves of amber hair

They dance

Buddy
I don't mean to pout
But any fool can see
I'm as good as dead
Without my bride-to-be
If the Lord should ask me
What would pacify
I would simply ask him
Send a Brenda Bly

So come on (Come on)
Fall in line and join the parade
So come on (Come on)
She's the reason Buddies were made
Everybody's rocking to the all-American

Girls ⎤
Stu ⎬ Everybody's rocking to the all-American
Wally ⎦
Buddy Everybody's rocking to the all-American boy
All Everybody's rocking to the all-American boy
Girls ⎤ Shoo-be-doo-be-wop
Stu ⎬ Shoo-be-doo-be-wop-wop
Wally ⎦ Shoo-be-doo-be-wop
Shoo-be-doo-be-wop-wop
Shoo-be-doo-be-wop
Shoo-be-doo-be-wop-wop
Wop-wop
Wop

Music No. 15a: Thief Underscore

Brenda Bly enters. She sees Buddy and turns cold

Brenda Well, nice to see someone has bounced back from the breakup of the decade.

Buddy What was that? You actually took a moment away from the case to realize we broke up?

Brenda My heart's broken into a million pieces, Buddy. In fact, I'm thinking about breaking into a rousing dance number myself.

Buddy That dance number was for you!

Brenda Well, you'll forgive me if I don't stick around for the encore. Some of us have better things to do with our time.

Brenda exits

Stu Ah, don't be so hard on yourself. You know she loves you, and as soon as she solves this case, she's gonna be running back into your arms.

Buddy That's it. I've got to solve the case myself. That's the one thing that's missing. Sure, she thinks I'm handsome. And it would take a blind deaf mute to miss all this charm. But what's the one thing missing?

Stu Humility?

Buddy Teen detective skills. Once I solve this case, she won't be able to keep her hands off me. (*He pulls Stu away from the others*) Stu, we're going back to that school tonight, and I'm going to solve that case.

Stu No, I won't do it.

Buddy But I need you. You've got to dress up like Madeline and distract Cecil for me.

Stu Buddy, he's all hands!

Buddy Don't you want Brenda and I to get back together?

Stu I won't do it. Under no circumstances will I go back to that place.

Jo Jo (*moving to Stu*) That's right. Stu's going out with me tonight.

Stu (*turning to Buddy*) What time you picking me up?

Buddy Eight o'clock sharp. Wear something pretty.

Buddy runs out. Bridget and Gidget run off after him

Stu heads for the exit but Jo Jo stops him

Jo Jo Hey, Stu. Where's the fire?

Stu I wish there were a fire. And I was trapped in the middle of it.

Jo Jo I don't know why you have to be so afraid of me. Just think of me as an old friend.

Stu Old friends don't offer hot oil massages.

Stu runs out

Jo Jo (*calling afer him*) You've been hanging out with the wrong friends!
Call me!

During the song, the singers move DL

   Wally takes the chairs and table off DR *and exits*

The US *curtains close and the Lights go down on the* US *area*

Music No. 16: Stu (*Jo Jo, Darcy, Autumn*)

        (*Singing*) Stu, what a pal
                He's a guy a gal depends on
                True
                His morale
                Isn't much to make new friends on
                He's awkward and he's shy
                His breath could use a mint
                So someone tell me why
                I think he's heaven sent
                Oo- oo-oo
                I'm crazy for—Stu
Autumn ⎤ Stu-doo-doo-wop, Stu-doo-doo-wop,
Darcy   ⎟ Stu-doo-doo-wop, Stoo -wop
Jo Jo   Stu, what a doll
                He's the kind girls call to cry to
                Who wouldn't fall
                For a face you couldn't lie to
                He rambles like a train
                He cannot sing in tune
                So someone please explain
                Why I think he hung the moon
                Oo-oo - oo
                I'm crazy for Stu
Autumn ⎤ Stu-doo-doo-wop, Stu-doo-doo-wop,
Darcy   ⎟ Stu-doo-doo-wop, Stoo -wop
Autumn   Some fellas drive
                They own their own car
                Come pick you up
                Wherever you are
                How Stu gets around

	About town
	He has found
	Another
Jo Jo	His mother
Autumn	Some men romance
	With roses and such
	Ask you to dance
	Not faint at the touch
Jo Jo	No man
	Ever can
	Stan or Dan
	Hold a candle to Stu
All	Stu! Stu! Stu!
	Stu! Stu! Stu! … Stu!
Jo Jo	Still he's a gem (gem)
	And I must have him beside me
	We'll sink or swim (swim)
	With the moon above to guide me
	He's got a crooked grin
	His hair is turning gray
	How happy we'll be then
	When he doesn't run away
	Oo-oo-oo
Autumn	That lazy swine
Jo Jo	Oo-oo-oo
	He's good as mine
	Oo-oo ——
	— oo
	I'm crazy for Stu

Music No. 16a: Playoff

Black-out

SCENE 3

Miss Van Strander's Office

The US *curtains open and the Lights come up* UC *revealing a desk and high-backed chair. Van Strander sits at the desk, motionless. She is still wearing her dark glasses. At first glance, she appears dead, but her snores reveal she's only sleeping*

Brenda Bly enters

Brenda Miss Van Strander.

Van Strander is startled. During the following, she tries to hide the fact that she is still having trouble seeing, occasionally delivering a line or gesture to the wrong place

Van Strander Great Caesar's ghost. You startled me.
Brenda You think *that's* scary. I actually *had* a run in with Great Caesar's ghost.
Van Strander Let me guess, Brenda Bly.
Brenda But in actuality it turned out to be a nasty troupe of madrigal singers out to sabotage a Renaissance Festival.
Van Strander Spare me, Miss Marbles. I've heard all about your adventures. Quite frankly, they bore me. A young girl like you shouldn't be wasting your time chasing goblins.
Brenda What would you suggest I do then, Miss Van Strander? What did you do when you were my age?

Van Strander is startled. Brenda has touched a nerve

Van Strander That's none of your business.
Brenda Did you ever have a passion?
Van Strander What part of "none of your business" do you not understand?
Brenda I don't understand any of it. I'm a nosy private eye, remember?
Van Strander Careful where you stick that nose, Brenda Bly.
Brenda I was just asking a simple question.

Music No. 16b: Underscore

I'm curious as to why you were so keen to shut down "Rocket Girl".
Van Strander What's this? You can't be serious? You are adding me to your list of suspects?
Brenda It's not as simple as all that. You see, when investigating a mystery, I prefer a process of elimination. Everyone's on the list of suspects, until I can clear them in any way.
Van Strander Do you ever shut up?
Brenda Take Madeline for example. She was running the spotlight at the time of the attack. Therefore, she couldn't have cut the rope from backstage. She's off the list. I would be more than happy to take your name off that list, if you can provide some sort of alibi and tell me why you were so against the show to begin with.

Van Strander Because it was an abomination! It puts an unsightly blemish on the school and on my reputation as headmistress.

Brenda Just how far would you go to make sure the show didn't go on, I wonder?

Van Strander Stick around, Brenda Bly. Stick around and find out. Now get out of my office! Out! Out!

Brenda exits

Music No. 17: Times Like These: Reprise *(Van Strander)*

> *(Singing)* Think you're so smart
> You know who's who
> Well Brenda Bly you ain't got a clue
> Don't be a fool girl
> It's cruel girl
> In times like these
> Watch as each star
> Rises and falls
> Now leading lady
> Your curtain calls
> Sha – do – wa – she— wop
> To be bop
> In times like these

Van Strander laughs an evil laugh, turns to exit, and walks straight into her desk. She regains her composure and slowly leaves the office, waving her arms in front of her

Music No. 17a: Scene Change/Underscore

The US curtains close and the Lights cross-fade to the DS area

SCENE 4

On the set of "Rocket Girl". The Moon

Autumn drags Darcy into the DS area in front of the US curtains. Darcy is now dressed in her space outfit

Autumn OK, now there is no need to panic. It is true that this is the last rehearsal before *Rocket Girl* opens to a live audience, and our leading lady couldn't even find her way to the theatre.

Darcy Gymnasiums and theatres really do look a lot alike.

Autumn But no matter. I wrote this part especially for you, and I am
convinced that you will not let me down. As soon as the music starts it'll
all start flowing back. Isn't that right?

Darcy That's absolutely right.

Autumn You're going to make us proud, aren't you?

Darcy Without a doubt.

Autumn And you're gonna rip into that role like there's no tomorrow?

Darcy I sure am.

Autumn Then let's do it.

Darcy Who am I playing again?

Autumn Rocket Girl. You are Rocket Girl. OK, let's take it from Rocket
Girl's arrival on the moon. Bridget and Gidget that's you.

Bridget
Gidget } (*off; together*) Ready.

Darcy But where do I stand?

Autumn Just do what comes naturally. I bet anything it'll come back to you.
And Rocket Girl lands on the moon. Curtain!

Music No. 18: All That and Cheese
(*Bridget, Gidget, Darcy and "Rocket Girl" cast*)

Autumn moves to the side of the stage to watch

The us *curtains open and the Lights come up on the* us *area. We are now on
the moon — a row of flats depicting craters has been placed along the back
of the set*

Darcy stands c, *with no clue what to do next*

Bridget and Gidget enter as tap-dancing space aliens

Bridget (*singing*)	Welcome stranger — come on in
Gidget	Take a load off — how ya been
Bridget } **Gidget** }	You've done more than sail those seven seas
Gidget	Need a shoulder — step right up
Bridget	Have a drink to pep you up
Bridget } **Gidget** }	You're our guest and we are here to please
Bridget	Never will you find a crater greater
Gidget	There's no gravity to bog down these

Bridget ⎤	Thank heavens
Gidget ⎦	There's a man here on the moon
	Made to make each moonie swoon
	Plus free parking
	All that and cheese

Jo Jo, Candy and other girls enter, also dressed as tap-dancing aliens

Throughout the following number, the girls try their best to push a clueless Darcy around the stage, constantly trying to put her in the right positions

Dance break

Bridget	There's no sun to make you sweat
Gidget	No hot summers here and yet
Bridget ⎤ **Gidget** ⎦	There's no snow to make your poor heart freeze
Gidget	All day long it's nice and cool
Bridget	Through the night the moon is full
Bridget ⎤ **Gidget** ⎦	Shooting stars create the nicest breeze
Gidget	That space ship can't find a better planet
All	Can it?
Bridget	If you're hungry — try take-out Chinese
All	No sushi
	Plus that man you're dreaming of
	Sure to set your course on love
Gidget	Live jazz nightly
All	All that and cheese
Bridget ⎤ **Gidget** ⎦	When back at home they ask what is it
All	Makes this place so nice to visit
	We're sure you'll say with ease
Bridget	Nothing too heinous
Gidget	Next stop Uranus
All	All that and cheese

The song ends. Everyone stands staring at Darcy. She just stares back blankly at them. Obviously, Darcy has the next line, but can't think of it. Eventually, she turns to Autumn

Darcy I'm sorry; I just don't remember any of this.

Van Strander enters from the wings

Van Strander Bad news, ladies. I'm *blind* and still I've never seen anything
so dreadful in all of my life.
Autumn I'll admit it needs a little work.
Van Strander The Hindenburg needed a little work. This piling heap needs
a miracle.
Gidget Or at least, a new leading lady. I'll play Rocket Girl. (*She takes the
helmet from Darcy*)
Bridget Who said Gidget gets to play Rocket Girl? Have you seen her act?
She makes Ethel Merman look subtle.
Gidget (*moving to Autumn*) Let me play the part, Autumn. I know the part
backwards and forwards.
Autumn I am not having this conversation.

Brenda enters from the wings, directly behind Van Strander

Brenda Wait a minute, Autumn. I find this pretty interesting.
Van Strander (*startled by Brenda's appearance*) You again!
Brenda Sorry, Miss Van Strander. It just seems only natural that one of the
twins takes over the lead.
Bridget Finally, someone is making some sense.
Brenda And what better reason for one of them to drop that sandbag on
Darcy's head?
Gidget How dare you?
Brenda It makes perfect sense.

Music No. 18a: Brenda Thinks

Twin sisters. Used to be the toast of Hollywood. You grew into your teens
and your career was at a standstill. Until now. This show would be a perfect
chance to shine again. If either of you could play the lead. The lead that
Darcy can no longer play.

The music stops; it starts again during the following

Bridget That does it. I'm calling my agent. (*She turns to Gidget*) Get Mom
on the phone.
Autumn How dare you sabotage my leading lady? She could have been a
star!
Bridget Oh, turn it off. You thought Darcy was dreadful a few days ago.
Darcy Autumn!
Autumn I did not.

Gidget You said she was playing the part like Shirley Temple after shock treatment!

Brenda Another interesting turn of events. Isn't it funny how suddenly, after the accident, you're so crazy about her doing the part?

Autumn I've always wanted her to do the part. Just look at her. She is Rocket Girl!

Brenda One of the major slip-ups of a nervous and paranoid criminal—after someone is bumped off, they pretend how much they loved the victim, so as to not be a suspect themselves.

The music stops

Autumn Brenda Bly, how dare you?

Brenda I'm sorry, Autumn, but no-one's above suspicion here. It's true, you weren't crazy about Darcy's performance two days ago.

Darcy Autumn!

Autumn That was just nerves speaking. I would have said that about any of the actresses. I'm a playwright. I'm insane.

Brenda Just how insane are you? That's the question.

Autumn I've had just enough out of you, Miss Snoopy Snoop. I'll show you. I'll bring Darcy's memory back and she'll open this show to rave reviews.

Brenda Let's hope so. If not, you might be writing your next play from a prison cell.

Autumn That does it. My next play is going to be about a busybody teen detective with large ankles! Come on, Darcy.

Autumn drags Darcy off

Van Strander watches with pleasure

Van Strander Don't fret, ladies. It's never too late to sign up for Home Ec.

Van Strander exits

The remaining girls descend upon Brenda

Gidget Brenda, you've got to find out who did this.

Jo Jo We can't do a proper show all the while knowing a maniac is on the loose.

Bridget Yeah, usually you've solved the case by now.

Brenda Well, I'm trying the best I can.

Jo Jo Try harder!

Gidget Stop worrying about Buddy so much and get on with the case!

Brenda I'm doing everything I can.
Bridget Obviously not everything. And quite frankly, I'm scared.
Brenda I'm scared too, Bridget. I was almost murdered myself.

The girls crowd around Brenda and prod her

Bridget Boo hoo. I've got industry people coming. If you don't solve the case, my career is history.
Gidget Not to mention your career as a teen detective!
Bridget Solve the case, Brenda Bly.
Jo Jo What are you waiting for?
Gidget I mean really. What are you waiting for? Christmas?
Brenda (*losing her temper and pushing the others away*) That's it! I have had enough! You think it's a cakewalk being a teen detective? Well, let me tell you, it's not. I've lost my boyfriend because of this stupid case! And if you want this maniac brought to justice, you're going to have to do it on your own! I'm quitting the teen detective business.

Brenda storms off

Everyone is left speechless. They stare after her

Bridget (*after a moment*) Did you see that? She *does* have large ankles.

Autumn runs back on stage

Autumn I did it! I hit Darcy over the head!
Gidget I knew it.
Autumn No, not before. Just now. I went a little insane after my run in with Brenda. I figured I'd hit Darcy over the head with a large object, and maybe that would bring back her memory.
Bridget And?

Music No. 19: Darcy's Memory Returns

Darcy (*off*)   On with my space suit
                        Off with a bang
                        I've packed my suitcase
                        Said goodbye to all the gang

Darcy enters with pride. The music swells. Everyone crowds around her to congratulate her

Gidget You remember it!

Darcy I remember it all. Thanks for hitting me over the head with that fire extinguisher. You're a true friend, Autumn. A true friend.
Autumn And that means that the show is back on without a hitch. Places everyone. From the top!

All the girls apart from Jo Jo run off in different directions

Jo Jo stands confused

Jo Jo But wait a minute. I think I've figured it out. Oh my God, I was an accomplice. Of course. Everyone, I know who dropped that sandbag on Darcy's head.

Of course, a sandbag falls directly on top of Jo Jo's head. She collapses

Autumn runs on stage

Autumn Shit.* (**or* "Doo doo" or "CUT!")*

Music No. 19a: Scene change/Underscore

The US *curtains close and the Lights fade* US

SCENE 5

The Costume Shop

The costume shop is set up or trucked on DR

The Lights come up DR. *Buddy paces back and forth in front of a costume rack*

Buddy Would you hurry up already?

Stu comes out from behind the costume rack, dressed again as Madeline

Stu You're gonna owe me big for this.
Buddy I would do it for you.
Stu No, you wouldn't.
Buddy Yes, I would.
Stu Fine, then you wear the dress. I'll snoop around.
Buddy You don't have any experience snooping around. I'm the one who used to date a teen detective, remember. I've decided that the first place to look for clues is Miss Van Strander's office.
Stu Out of the pan, into the fire.

Buddy She has all the records. Records of all the girls that go here. That should clue me in.

Stu And what am I supposed to do?

Buddy Distract Cecil.

Stu How do you even know I'm going to run into him?

Buddy I left him a note, asking him to meet you up here.

Stu You didn't.

Cecil (*calling, off*) Hallo, Madeline.

Buddy I did. (*He hides behind the costume rack*)

Cecil enters

Cecil Madeline.

Stu *Bonjour!*

Cecil Spare me, Frenchy McFrench. I'm running low on patience tonight, and I don't have time to hear a load from the likes of you.

Buddy takes a jacket, glasses and cap that look just like Cecil's from the costume rack. He stands behind Cecil, checks himself out and exits

Stu Uh, no speakie English.

Cecil You think I was born yesterday, Marie Antoin--*not!* I know who you are.

Stu You do?

Cecil See this badge. With this badge comes knowledge.

Stu Shiny.

Cecil I know your dirty little secret. You think you can pull a fast one over Cecil Sessille?

Stu I don't want to pull anything.

Cecil I know you speak English.

Stu Mama.

Cecil Putting on this poor, helpless little act. Poor little French girl, all the way over from Gay Paree. "Ooh la la. Look at me, I'm French." All to get me wrapped up in your spell.

Stu Funny, no?

Cecil No. No funny. And I'll tell you why. Because you're messing with a man who's already spoken for. See? There's another love in my life. She carries the torch to my heart. How dare you tempt me with your European ways and that love poem?

Stu Poem?

Cecil Oh, you're a naughty little French girl, aren't ya? I think you *do* deserve a spanking, just like you wrote in that note you left me.

Stu Buddy, you're a dead man!

Cecil Who's Buddy?

Stu You're my buddy. Aren't you?

Cecil Oh, am I ever? No! What am I doing? I'm spoken for. My heart belongs to another.

Stu But how will I go on?

Cecil You have to forget this ever happened. It'll be painful, of course. You'll hear a song on the radio, and you'll think of me. And weep.

Stu I'm weeping already.

Cecil You just got to do what I do. Wake up in the morning, drag yourself out of that bed, put one foot in front of the other.

Stu Not so easy in these heels.

Cecil Me? I look myself in the mirror, and I say "Cecil, this is only temporary. You're not gonna be a security guard for the rest of your life, by cracky! You're gonna make something of yourself." And so are you, Frenchy. You don't need the lies. You don't need the deceit, or smutty poems.

Stu Smutty?

Cecil All you need is belief in yourself. And maybe a heavier foundation. (*He heads for the exit*)

Stu You can't go.

Cecil I gotta. I can't stay with you one second longer. I've got to be strong.

Music No. 20: Undercover (*Stu and Cecil*)

Stu realizes that he has no choice. He strikes a seductive pose

Stu But it isn't safe. And poor Madeline is frightened. She is shaking. You want to feel Madeline shake?

Cecil Oh, do I. But I gotta go.

Stu No!

	(*Singing*) A shrouded figure waits outside that door
	He's tasted blood and now come back for more
	It's times like these when life is do or die
	So do it with me — you got an alibi
Stu ⎫	Let's go undercover
Cecil ⎭	Let's get down below
	Once we're undercover
Stu	Discover a clue you really ought to know

The US *curtains open and the Lights cross-fade* US *to reveal Van Strander's office, denoted by the desk and high-backed chair as previously. As yet unseen, Van Strander is sitting in the chair with its back to the audience*

Buddy enters dressed as Cecil. He sneaks over to the desk

Van Strander whirls around in the high-backed chair

Van Strander I waited for you for two hours last night. You never showed.

Buddy Oh, yah, that must have been a mistake. I thought you were meeting me at my place.

Van Strander Don't play games with my heart, Cecil Sessille. I've had my heart broken before. This old ticker can't take another breakdown.

Buddy No, honey — doll-face — thingy. I would never break your heart. I love ya.

Van Strander Then prove it.

Buddy I was afraid you were gonna ask for proof.

Van Strander But not here. Meet me back in my place. Don't keep me waiting.

Van Strander exits

Buddy watches her go and starts looking through her drawers

The Lights come up on Cecil and Stu

Cecil (*singing*) There's danger lurking everywhere we turn
                 But down below my yearning embers burn
                 Who gets it next we'll have to wait and see
                 The screaming tonight is gonna come from me

Stu   ⌈ Let's go undercover
Cecil ⌋ Let's both disappear
          Once we're undercover

Cecil   Hold on to me tight — there's not a thing to fear. (*He goes for Stu*)

Stu (*speaking*) No, please!

Cecil I thought this is what you wanted.

Stu I do. Just not here. Someone could walk in.

Cecil Ah, you want somewhere more private, do ya.

Stu And dark. Very dark.

Cecil I know just the place.

Cecil drags Stu out of the costume shop and towards Van Strander's office. As they get closer to the office, Buddy hears them approaching

Buddy Oh no! Somebody's coming. (*He hides behind the desk*)

Stu ⌉   ⌈ Let's go undercover
Cecil (*singing*) Let's get down below
                     Once we're undercover
Stu   Discover a clue you really ought to know

Cecil pursues Stu round the desk. Buddy crawls around on his hands and knees to avoid them. By the end of the next section of the song, Stu is lying on Van Strander's desk with Cecil about to climb on him

Stu ⎱ **Cecil** ⎰	Let's go undercover Let's both disappear Once we're undercover
Cecil	Hold on to me tight — you oughta
Stu	Hold on to me tight — you gotta
Cecil ⎱ **Stu** ⎰	Hold on to me tight — there's not a thing to fear

Buddy stands up from behind the desk

Cecil (*speaking*) What the hell are you doing in here?

Van Strander enters carrying her sunglasses. She is ecstatic

Van Strander Cecil! I can see! It's a miracle. I can see!
Cecil Vera!
Van Strander (*shocked to see a young girl lying on top of her desk*) Cecil? Who is she?
Cecil Trust me. It's not as bad as it looks.

Stu sits up. His wig falls off

Van Strander No kidding.
Cecil What the ...
Van Strander You're a monster, Cecil Sessille. A monster!

Van Strander runs out of the office

Cecil I'll deal with you two later. Vera! Vera!!

Cecil runs off after Van Strander

Buddy What do you think you're doing?
Stu I was distracting Cecil like you asked.
Buddy You were supposed to keep him *away* from the office.
Stu It was the only place we could have privacy.
Buddy You're a very complex man, aren't you?
Stu It doesn't matter. You're in the office now.
Buddy I am. Quick, before they come back.

Buddy rummages through the desk drawers

Stu My hair must be a mess.

Music No. 20a: Buddy and Stu Discover

Buddy (*finding a newspaper clipping in a file*) What's this? (*He shows the clipping to Stu*) Oh, no, my suspicions were right. Look, Van Strander used to be an actress.
Stu So?
Buddy So, don't you see? If *she* wasn't going to be a star, *no-one was.*
Stu Van Strander!

The Lights snap out on Buddy and Stu. The US *curtains close*

A small group of detectives enters with flashlights and crosses the stage

Music No. 20b: Brenda Bly: Teen Detective: Reprise

Detectives   A play in disarray
                        Van Strander in a snit
                        To everyone's dismay
                        Our saviour up and quit
                        There's no-one left to douse this raging fire
                        Did Brenda pick the wrong time to retire?
                        Left to dry with no directive
                        Bring me my
                        Teen Detective
                        Teen Detective
                        Teen Detective
                        Teen Detective

Scene 6

The Hospital

The US *curtains open and the Lights come up on the* US *area to reveal the hospital setting as in Act I Scene 3*

The girls—Darcy, Madeline, Bridget, Gidget, Candy and others, all except Jo Jo and Autumn—pace in the waiting room

Autumn enters

Autumn Ladies, could I have your attention please? Unfortunately, Jo Jo is still knocked out cold. The doctors are sure she's going to be all right, but it looks like she won't be able to make the show this evening. A little on the unprofessional side if you ask me. But nevertheless, I've made a few alterations. The role of General Flavaven will now be played by Madeline Foom-du-la-quack-quack. Whatever her last name is.

Darcy But she can't speak a word of English.

Autumn Luckily, Jo Jo was so desperate not to play a man, she has already taught Madeline the part phonetically. (*She turns to Madeline*) Show 'em, Madeline.

Madeline steps forward

Madeline (*reciting slowly and loudly*) Laydeez an Genelmen, membears of zee press, Monsieur Le Prezidonte. I proudly gives you *Rochette Grill*.

Nurse Wilder enters, still with her stethoscope stuck in her ears

Autumn stops Nurse Wilder

Autumn Excuse me.

Nurse Wilder (*shouting*) Yes!

Autumn Could you give me any more information on Jo Jo Reynolds?

Nurse Wilder (*shouting*) I'll need the patient's name.

Autumn I just gave her your name.

Nurse Wilder (*shouting*) Now you're just talking in riddles.

Autumn pulls the stethoscope out of Nurse Wilder's ears

Autumn Could I talk to a doctor?

Nurse Wilder Sure, honey. I'll just need you to fill out some paper work, and we'll get someone to take a look at ya.

Autumn (*throwing up her arms in defeat and turning to the other girls*) Oh, forget it. I don't know what I was thinking. Don't you see the stars are working against me? It's over.

Nurse Wilder Didn't you read the sign? There is no crying allowed on my shift.

Autumn What sign?

Nurse Wilder Well, it's inside my locker, but the rule applies just the same. Nothing is so bad that you can't shake it off. Come on, do like Nurse Wilder. (*She shakes wildly for quite a long time*)

The girls stare at Nurse Wilder. Finally, she stops shaking and looks at
Autumn

See, I feel a hundred percent better.
Autumn Van Strander was right. Life is a tapestry of disappointment. I
know when I've been defeated. Come on, girls.

Autumn takes a deep breath and heads for the exit. The girls sadly follow
right behind her. Nurse Wilder stops her

Music No. 21: Oogie Woogie Boogie (*Nurse Wilder and Company*)

Nurse Wilder   So you're feeling mighty low down
                        Ev'ry dice you roll you lose
                        Your poor spirit's feeling so down
                        You're drownin' in those old town blues
                        Well, there's a little dance
                        I'm thinking of
                        That'll chase those clouds of grey
                        Let's do the oogie woogie boogie
                        Honey chase those clouds away

                        Wave your hands in the air
Girls   Shack a doo-shack a doo
Nurse Wilder   Turn your toes inside out
Girls   Mack a doo-mack a doo
Nurse Wilder   Shake your hips here and there
Girls   One two-one two
Nurse Wilder   Don't stand there and pout
Girls   Boo hoo
Nurse Wilder   Honey, it's all about
                        The oogie woogie boogie

                        So you think the sky is falling
                        Ev'ry chance you take you fail
                        But why stand there sad and bawlin'
                        You could be shaking that there tail
                        Well, there's a little dance
                        I'm thinking of
                        That'll help you pass the time
                        Let's do the oogie woogie boogie
                        If we don't then that's a crime

Nurse Wilder	Wave your hands in the air
Girls	Shack a doo — shack a doo
Nurse Wilder	Turn your toes inside out
Girls	Mack a doo — mack a doo
Nurse Wilder	Shake your hips here and there
Girls	One two — one two
Nurse Wilder	Don't stand there and pout
Girls	Boo hoo
Nurse Wilder	Honey, it's all about
	The oogie woogie boogie

Creepy crawlies get ya
And fill your heart with fright
But teach them creeps the oogie
And oogie woogie boogie throughout the night

	Wave your hands in the air
Girls	Shack a doo — shack a doo
Nurse Wilder	Turn your toes inside out
Girls	Mack a doo — mack a doo
Nurse Wilder	Shake your hips here and there
Girls	One two — one two
Nurse Wilder	Don't stand there and pout
Girls	Boo hoo
Nurse Wilder	Honey, it's all about
	The oogie woogie boogie

Dance break

During the dance break, Jo Jo is wheeled out in a wheelchair

Nurse Wilder does a crazy healing dance around Jo Jo. Jo Jo leaps up from the wheelchair and joins the dancing

All	Creepy crawlies get ya
	And fill your heart with fright
	But teach them creeps the oogie
	And oogie woogie boogie throughout the night

	Wave your hands in the air
Nurse Wilder	Shack a doo — shack a doo
Girls	Turn your toes inside out
Nurse Wilder	Mack a doo — mack a doo

Girls	Shake your hips here and there
Nurse Wilder	One two — one two
Girls	Don't stand there and pout
Nurse Wilder	Boo hoo
Girls	Honey, it's all about
All	The oogie woogie boogie

Autumn and the Girls are in much better spirits

Autumn (*turning to Nurse Wilder*) Thank you, Nurse. You're absolutely
   right. If you want something bad enough, you do have to fight for it.
Nurse Wilder Darn right, you do.
Autumn What are we waiting for? Now that Jo Jo's better, the show is going
   to go off without a hitch.
Jo Jo I'm sorry. Do I know you?
Autumn Not another case of amnesia!
Nurse Wilder It's going around. But don't worry. Nurse Wilder is here.
   She'll make everything better.

Nurse Wilder puts her arms around the girls and heads for the exit

   Dr Sniffles enters and stands in front of Nurse Wilder

Dr Sniffles Mrs Wilder, for the last time — you are not an employee here.
   You are a patient.

Nurse Wilder starts shaking again

   I need you to give me back the lab coat, and go back to your room. Mrs
   Wilder?

   Nurse Wilder stops shaking and runs off stage. Dr Sniffles follows

Autumn I knew it was too good to be true. We were taking advice from a
   crazy lady.
Darcy She may be crazy, but she still has a point.
Autumn No, she doesn't have a point. The show is over. It's dead.

   Nurse Ivy and other members of the hospital staff enter

   You hear me? Dead!
Nurse Ivy I'm sorry. We did everything we could.

Buddy and Stu run in and pull Autumn and Darcy away from the crowd

Buddy Girls, we need your help.
Darcy Do I know you?
Buddy It's Buddy and Stu.
Autumn Well, that explains everything. I always thought you two were a little too close.
Stu We're in disguise.
Buddy I've got to talk to Brenda. Do you know where she is?
Darcy She got a call from Miss Van Strander asking her to meet her at her remote cabin in the woods.
Buddy We've got to get her. Quick.
Stu Buddy, I'm in heels.
Buddy I've got to save my girlfriend.
Stu Fine. Let's go.

Buddy and Stu run off stage

The Lights change

Music No. 21a: Scene Change

Everyone exits

The following set change can be accomplished by the detectives with flashlights: the hospital setting is removed and replaced either by a truck with a cabin setting on it or simply by an old armchair and a side table with, maybe, a window flown in. On the table are a bottle of whiskey and a framed portrait of Van Strander's mother

While this is happening we see Brenda on her way to the woods with Buddy and Stu in hot pursuit. They exit

Scene 7

A Remote Cabin in the Woods

Music No. 22: Van Strander's Lament (*Van Strander*)

The Lights come up US on the cabin. It is night. Moonlight floods in through the window. Crickets can be heard. Van Strander is sitting in the armchair, glass of whiskey in hand

Van Strander (*singing*) Every morning, every day I see the same old sight
Girls who dream and drown inside their folly
From the break of day
And well beyond the dark of night
Chasing showbiz like a lovesick collie
But they'll learn one day their dream comes with a wrench
And the smell of greasepaint always leaves a stench.
(*She takes a swig of whiskey*)

Brenda Bly enters, framed in the doorway if there is one. Moonlight floods into the cabin

Brenda You wanted to see me, Miss Van Strander?
Van Strander Yes, welcome to my remote cabin in the woods. I hope you didn't have trouble finding it.
Brenda Oh no. Actually, I was once abducted and held hostage in the cabin just across the lake.
Van Strander Isn't that lucky? Small world. Would you care for a nice hot cup of cocoa?
Brenda I really shouldn't. It'll keep me up all night.
Van Strander Oh, just a little cup won't kill you.
Brenda Miss Van Strander, do you mind me asking why you needed to see me out here at your remote cabin in the woods?
Van Strander I invited you out because I wanted to discuss the case with you.
Brenda I'm not on the case any more.
Van Strander Do you mind me asking why not?
Brenda It just caused too much mess. I'm a young girl, in my prime. I should be enjoying life.
Van Strander Enjoying life is for suckers, Brenda Bly. Suckers and people who have nothing better to do. And now Brenda Bly, I have something for you.

Van Strander stands and moves behind the chair. She suddenly pulls out —
a photo album

Brenda What's this?
Van Strander My scrapbook. (*She opens it*)
Brenda (*looking at the book*) My goodness, what a beautiful young woman.
Van Strander Yes.
Brenda Where are you?
Van Strander That *is* me.
Brenda But this is a production still. You were an actress?

Van Strander (*singing*) I'd be the star beyond compare
                In life I would get ahead
                My mamma said
                A life with sunshine in the room
                I'd soar if I only tried
                She lied
                I'd be the rich one centre stage
                Not be the bitch one that's filled with rage
                To be so bitter at my age
                For God's sake — someone kill me

                There was a man who held my hand
                And said that he'd share my bed
                My husband said
                A life with roses in full bloom
                He'd stay there right by my side
                He lied

                He said how perfect our life would be
                He swore the world he'd give to me
                But in the end
                I got VD
                No kidding — someone kill me*

                [*Alternative lyric:
                He was so young with hopes on high
                A bit high strung but so was I
                And then he hung me out to dry
                No kidding — someone kill me]

Van Strander sinks into the chair and reaches for the picture of her mother

                Mamma I got my drama
Brenda What happened to this man?
Van Strander He was jealous, of my career. He couldn't stand the idea of
   so many people adoring me and fawning all over me. He wanted that part
   exclusively.
Brenda And you gave it up?
Van Strander Every bit of it. The lights. The glamour. The ditsy chorus
   queens. It was all gone in an instant. And the only thing left is in that book.
   And through the years, that beautiful star turned into a bitter, hard woman.
   (*She grabs Brenda by the shoulders*). Don't turn into me, Brenda Bly. You
   need to follow your heart. Don't just enjoy life! *Embrace* life doing the

one thing you were put on this planet to do. And if Buddy is the man for you, then he'll allow for that. It's 1958. Anything is possible. Good God, we are going to send someone to the moon.

Brenda The moon! Yes, of course. Why didn't I think of it earlier? I've got to go. I've got a case to crack!

Brenda hands the photo album back to Van Strander and moves DS. *Van Strander waves her off happily*

The US *curtains close on Van Strander and the Lights cross-fade to the* DS *area*

Music No. 23: Back on the Case (*Brenda*)

> (*Singing*) Go tell a flower she's a bird
> No matter how hard you try
> She'll never fly
> But tell that flower she can bloom
> The very next thing you know
> She'll grow
> Don't tell a moonbeam that it's a star
> Don't tell a rocket that it's a car
> Just let us all be who we are
> Me I'm a teen detective

A Cool Dude drives up in a cut-out cool convertible and stops

(*Speaking*) Get me to the Whitney Ellis School for Girls. And step on it!

Brenda hops into the back seat. Cool Dude drives, and Brenda swerves and bounces as they go

> (*Singing*) Go tell a kite to stay aground
> And no matter what you prove
> He'll never move
> But give that kite a running start
> And just like the day before
> He'll soar
> And watch him travel to worlds unknown
> Up past the heavens all on his own
> Just like I will after I've shown
> That I'm a teen detective

The Cool Dude comes to a stop. Brenda gets out of the car, and waves to him

(*Speaking*) Thanks!

Brenda runs off

There is the sound effect of the car revving up; it speeds off stage

The Lights cross-fade to the US *area*

The US *curtains open slightly, enough to reveal Brenda at the front of a ship (represented by two panels that make up the sloping sides of the prow) flanked by two sailors standing at attention. Brenda leans out towards the water; the wind blows her perfectly coiffed hair. During the following verse, Brenda and the sailors sway*

Brenda (*singing*) And one day soon
                 We'll reach the moon
                 Up past the sky
                 My guy and I
                 And one day we will win the race
                 Back on the case
                 And in the place where I belong

Brenda picks up two ski poles from behind the panels

The sailors pick up the panels and exit L *and* R *with them*

Brenda is now snow-skiing down a mountain slope; fake snow is blown about her face from behind the US *curtains*

                 Go tell the sun that he's the moon
                 The very next day you'll see
                 It's not to be
                 But get him in the light of day
                 As sure as the world is mine
                 He'll shine
                 Don't keep him locked up inside some tomb
                 Go give a flower a chance to bloom
                 And let a kite fly with lots of room
                 Just like a teen detective

The US *curtains open fully to reveal the backstage area, with the costume rack, rocket ship and various flats*

Brenda proudly tosses her ski poles to the side, dusts the snow off her shoulders as if this is an everyday occurrence, then marches DC

The Lights come up DC

                 I'll get my man.

SCENE 8

On Stage/Backstage

Darcy runs in and taps Brenda on the shoulder

Darcy Brenda. Shhh!! The show's about to start.
Brenda Sorry, Darcy. What do you mean the show's about to start?
Darcy I got my memory back.

Autumn enters, darting quickly across the stage

Autumn Places, ladies. We open in five minutes.

Autumn exits

Brenda Darcy, before the sandbag fell on your head, what did you do with
your camera?
Darcy It was around my neck. But someone must have taken it off after I
was knocked out because I haven't seen it since.
Brenda Of course they took it off. There would have been plenty of
commotion to slip it off without anyone noticing.
Darcy Why would someone want my camera?
Brenda I think you took a picture on the field trip that our little culprit would
like to keep undeveloped. I'll be right back.

Music No. 23a: Darcy's Capture

Brenda runs off

Darcy stands in confusion. The Lights dim

Darcy What do I do in the meantime?

We hear a noise off stage

Hallo? Hallo? Is anybody there?

*A figure in black (Madeline, as yet unrecognizable in a ski mask) enters
from behind Darcy R, covers her mouth with a chloroformed pad and drags
her off*

SCENE 9

The Prop Room

The US *curtains close and the prop room setting is set up or trucked on* DL

The Lights cross-fade to the prop room to reveal Darcy, tied and gagged, sitting in a chair. Madeline, still unrecognizable in black, stands right at the edge of the acting area, almost off stage

Brenda Bly enters carrying a handgun and, in her US *hand, Darcy's camera. She does not see the figure in black*

Brenda Darcy, I've been looking all over for you.

Darcy tries to get Brenda's attention with her eyes, to warn her of the danger

I figured out who attacked you. They didn't want to keep you from being in the play. They wanted to stop you from developing those pictures.

Madeline slowly sneaks up behind Brenda. Darcy shakes her head

Oh, yes. No need to shake your head at me. I'm Brenda Bly: Teen Detective. I had a hunch who that person was and just searched their locker. And look what I found! (*She holds up the camera*)

Darcy screams underneath the gag

No need to thank me, Darcy. That's what friends are for. (*She takes the gag out of Darcy's mouth*)
Darcy Behind you.

Madeline grabs the gun out of Brenda's hand. Brenda swirls around and faces her

Brenda I was wondering how long it was going to take you to grab the gun, Madeline. But that's not your real name at all, is it?

Madeline takes off her ski mask. She now speaks in a Russian accent

Madeline Brenda Bly: Teen Detective. Your reputation suits you well.
Brenda Too bad I can't say the same about your outfit.
Darcy I'm confused.

Brenda She's not a foreign exchange student from France, Darcy. She's a Russian spy from ... well, Russia.

Madeline Very good, indeed. My real name is Oxanna. But how did you figure it out?

Brenda Simple. When Jo Jo mentioned Jerry Lewis earlier, you didn't flinch. You acted as if you didn't even know who he was.

Madeline I don't. Who's this Jerry Lewis you keep going on about?

Brenda That was your biggest mistake. Everyone knows that all French people love Jerry Lewis. He's the equivalent of Elvis Presley.

Darcy Are you serious?

Brenda I know. French. There's no accounting for taste. And then I realized that Darcy's camera was missing, and it made me wonder. What kind of pictures were on that camera that we couldn't see?

Darcy I was just experimenting. There was the full-length mirror. You would have done the same.

Brenda Not those pictures. I'm talking about these! (*She pulls a stack of photographs out of the waistband of her skirt and gives it to Darcy*)

Darcy looks at the pictures

Darcy There we are at Cape Canaveral, outside the decompression chamber.

Brenda But look behind you. Madeline slipping top secret blueprints into her own bag.

Madeline How did you develop those so quickly!

Brenda Last summer I went to photography camp.

Madeline Of course you did.

Brenda You see, Darcy, she was terrified that your pictures would blow her cover.

Darcy But she couldn't have dropped the sandbag on my head. She was operating the spotlight.

Brenda But she wasn't at all. Remember Jo Jo was so desperate not to be General Flavaven that she had taught Madeline the part. At the time of your attack, Jo Jo was running the spotlight, and Madeline was backstage, about to go on as General Flavaven.

Madeline Vell, done. Vell done indeed. Yes, it was too easy to believe. There are lesser spies who break into science labs, or climb walls into deadly fortresses. Me, I go on field trip, steal secret plans, and now send Russia to the moon before the stinky Americans.

Music No. 24: Next Stop: The Moon: Reprise (*Madeline*)

Madeline laughs manically

(*Singing*) One fine day the USA

Would sail beyond the stars
Thanks to this here Russian spy
That time instead is ours
So just ahead
A brand new world
It's up up and away
We're gonna see the galaxy
Before the USA

Who needs your baseball
Or apple pie
Thanks to Oxanna
We are heading to the sky
And that stinky Elvis Presley
Guess what? He sings off tune
See ya soon suckers

Voices (*off*)   Ah! Ah! Ah!
Madeline   Next stop the moon.
(She laughs manically and points the gun back at them on the button of the number. Speaking) And now you vill kindly give me the photographs?
Brenda And if I don't give them to you?
Madeline I vill shoot you.
Brenda And if I do give them to you?
Madeline I vill shoot you.
Brenda Either way ...
Madeline I vill shoot you.
Darcy They really like Jerry Lewis?
Brenda Darcy!
Madeline Enough of this chitchat. Give me the photos.
Brenda If I'm going to die either way, then I choose dying for my country. I won't give them to you.
Madeline Fine. Brenda Bly: Teen Idiot. Have it your vay.
Darcy Where do I stand in this whole situation? You get the pictures, you don't get the pictures. How does it look for me?
Madeline I vill shoot you.
Brenda You're going to have to go through me first.

Brenda runs to Darcy and stands close in front of her

Darcy You're such a good friend, Brenda. Such a good friend. Ooh, and your hair smells nice.
Brenda Thank you. I just washed it.
Madeline Enough, I say. Give me the photos or you both die.

Brenda Well, you can't blame a girl for trying. Here.

Music No. 24a: The Conclusion

Brenda tosses the pictures high in the air towards Madeline. As Madeline reaches for the pictures, Brenda grabs the gun

Not so smart now, are you, Oxanna?

Buddy and Stu enter with Van Strander who is tied up and gagged

Buddy Brenda, I did it! I solved the case. It was the awful Miss Van Strander. Not only is she a sadistic shrew, but she's a homicidal maniac as well. *(He takes the gun from Brenda)*
Brenda Buddy, I ——
Buddy Don't be scared, Brenda. I've got it all under control. Madeline, hold this. *(He hands Madeline the gun)*
Brenda ⎫
Darcy ⎭ *(together)* No!
Madeline But yes! *(She points the gun at the others)*
Brenda Buddy, it's not Van Strander. It's Madeline.

Jo Jo enters

Jo Jo Guys, I got my memory back.
Madeline Freeze!
Jo Jo You know what? I've had just about enough out of you.

Jo Jo takes the gun out of Madeline's hands. Brenda takes it from Jo Jo

Brenda Well, the tables have turned again, haven't they?
Madeline You vant to kill me? You haven't got the guts.
Brenda What do we think guys?
All Shoot her. Shoot her.

Cecil runs on

Cecil I'll teach you boys to sneak into an all-girl school! *(He sees Brenda holding a gun and takes it from her)* Hey, that's no toy!

Madeline grabs the gun from Cecil and points it at the others

Brenda Now do you see why I work alone?

Madeline You may vork alone, but you vill die together. Jo Jo, thank you
so much for letting me stay in your room. However, you snore. I vill kill
you first.
Stu No! (*He jumps between Madeline and Jo Jo*)
Jo Jo Stu, you do care!
Madeline (*moving to Van Strander*) Then how about the sadistic shrew?
Van Strander That name's gonna stick, I just know it.
Cecil (*jumping in front of Van Strander*) You'll have to go through me first.
Van Strander Cecil!
Madeline (*moving to Brenda*) Then that leaves Brenda Bly: Teen Detective.
Buddy (*jumping in front of Brenda*) Over my dead body.
Madeline Done.
Brenda No!

*Madeline puts her finger on the trigger to shoot Buddy. Brenda jumps in front
of him. Madeline shoots. In slow motion, Brenda collapses to the floor*

Buddy Brenda! (*He makes to run to Brenda*)

*Madeline steps over Brenda's body and threatens everyone with the gun,
forcing them together*

Madeline Get back. All of you. Where is your teen detective now?
Brenda (*jumping up and tapping Madeline on the shoulder*) Behind you.

*Madeline spins around. Brenda attacks Madeline. They struggle for the gun.
Eventually, Brenda takes the gun*

Voices (*off*)   Brenda Bly
                            Teen Detective.
Brenda This is a prop room, Oxanna! What kind of spy can't tell the
difference between a real gun and a prop?
Madeline I hate showbiz.
Cecil Well, you're gonna be singing like a canary down at FBI. Come with
me, Ruskie. Your days at Whitney Ellis are over.
Van Strander And don't think you're getting a refund on your tuition.

Cecil exits with Madeline. Autumn runs in

Autumn Could someone please tell me what the heck is going on back here?
Darcy Madeline was a Russian spy, but Brenda caught her.
Jo Jo We were nearly killed in cold blood.
Autumn Hallo? I have a show opening in a matter of seconds.

Darcy But Jo Jo just got out of the hospital. Is she well enough to go on?
Jo Jo It depends. Who would I be playing?
Autumn General Flavaven.
Jo Jo Stu, hold me. I'm not well.
Brenda I've got a perfect idea. Let Miss Van Strander do it.

Music No. 25: Underscore and Finale

Van Strander What?
Brenda Remember? Embrace life, doing the one thing you were put on this
planet to do.
Van Strander I couldn't possibly.
Autumn Fine. Jo Jo, you have to go on.
Van Strander Over my dead body!

Darcy, Autumn and Van Strander exit

The US curtains close

Jo Jo You saved my life.
Stu No, I didn't.
Jo Jo You did. You were going to take a bullet for me.
Stu No, I wasn't.
Jo Jo This is going to be the best thing that ever happened to you, Stu. Just
you wait and see. As soon as you fall in love with me, you're not going to
know what hit you.

Stu and Jo Jo exit

Buddy Brenda, I'm so sorry. I should have never come between you and teen
detecting.
Brenda No, I'm sorry. Of course, you would never be attracted to Van
Strander. How could I miss something so obvious?
Buddy Then you're my girl again?
Brenda I'm absolutely your girl again. Case closed.
Buddy } *(singing)* Though we found every clue
Brenda } It was tough pulling through
                        Even so I always knew
                        I'd (you'd) end up with my (your) man

Jo Jo and Stu enter holding hands

Jo Jo }   Even under such stress
Stu }   I (you) won't settle for less

Personal: **Darcy**: camera
                Brenda: bus keys

SCENE 2

Set: US of curtains
                Sign saying "Rocket Girl: Inaugural Flight to the Moon"

Strike: Sign
                Rack of costumes

Off stage: Clipboards (**Girls** as **Scientists**)
                Sandbag on a rope (**Stage Management**)

Personal: **Brenda**: flashlight

SCENE 3

Set: Sign with "Maternity" and "Morgue" on it
                Folding hospital screen

Strike: Sign
                Sandbag

Off stage: Hospital charts (**Dr Sniffles**)

Personal: **Dr Sniffles**: large syringe

SCENE 4

Set: Costume rack or two
                Few flats

Strike: Sign
                Screen

Off stage: Bottle of wine (**Cecil**)

SCENE 5

Re-set: Spaceship flat

Strike: Flats and costume rack

Off stage: Large can of red paint and brush (**Autumn**)

SCENE 6

Set: Costumed mannequin
                 Bolts of fabric
                 Large trunk
                 Various theatrical props

Off stage: Large sword (**Brenda**)
                 Mirrorball (**Stage Management**)

SCENE 7

No additional props

SCENE 8

During scene change p. 38

Set: Black camera strap

Strike: Costume shop props

ACT II

SCENE 1

No additional props

SCENE 2

Set: Soda shop counter with glasses etc.
                 Small table
                 Two chairs
                 Juke box
                 Sign saying "McFrosties"

SCENE 3

Set: US of curtains
                 Desk. *In a drawer*: file containing newspaper clipping
                 High-backed chair

Strike: Soda shop setting

SCENE 4

Set: US of curtains
                   Row of flats depicting craters

Strike: Desk
                   High-backed chair

SCENE 5

No additional props

SCENE 6

Personal: **Nurse Wilder**: stethoscope

SCENE 7

During scene change p. 67

Set: US of curtains
                   Old armchair
                   Side table. *On it*: bottle of whiskey, glass, framed portrait of **Van
                       Strander**'s mother
                   Window
                   Photograph album

Strike: Hospital setting from ACT II, SCENE 6

Off stage: Wheelchair (**Jo Jo**)
                   Cut-out cool convertible (**Cool Dude**)

During scene change p.71

Set: US of curtains
                   Two panels to make up ship's prow
                   Two ski poles

SCENE 8

Personal: **Madeline**: pad (for chloroform)

SCENE 9

Set: Chair

Off stage: Handgun (**Brenda**)

Personal: **Darcy**: ropes and gag
                   Brenda: stack of photographs
                   Van Strander: ropes and gag

LIGHTING PLOT

ACT I

To open: House lights on; darkness on stage

Cue 1	Girl's ear-piercing scream *House lights snap off*	(Page 1)
Cue 2	Music begins. When ready *Bring up lights on* US *area*	(Page 1)
Cue 3	The US curtains close *Cross-fade to* DS *area*	(Page 1)
Cue 4	**All**:"Teen Detective" *Cross-fade to* US *area*	(Page 2)
Cue 5	The US curtains close *Cross-fade to* DS *area*	(Page 2)
Cue 6	**All**:"And do it all in heels" *Cross-fade to* US *area*	(Page 3)
Cue 7	The girls defeat the **Mad Groundskeeper** *Cross-fade to* DS *area*	(Page 3)
Cue 8	**All**: "Teen Detective" *Black-out*	(Page 3)
Cue 9	Everyone except **Brenda Bly** exits *Bring up lights* DS	(Page 4)
Cue 10	Freestanding sign is set *Bring up bright general exterior lighting*	(Page 4)
Cue 11	**Girls**: "The Sixties might bring" *Cross-fade to school stage lighting*	(Page 6)
Cue 12	The **Girls** pose for a picture *Flash*	(Page 7)

Cue 13   US curtains close   (Page 7)
          Fade lights on US area

Cue 14   **Autumn** takes a picture   (Page 8)
          Flash

Cue 15   US curtains open   (Page 9)
          Bring up lights on US area

Cue 16   **Darcy** moves C and takes a pose   (Page 13)
          Bring up spotlight on backdrop

Cue 17   **Darcy**: "Me! On me!"   (Page 13)
          Move spotlight to light **Darcy**

Cue 18   **Darcy**: "Next stop the ..."   (Page 13)
          Strobe light

Cue 19   Music stops   (Page 13)
          Return lights to Cue 17 state

Cue 20   All but **Brenda** exit   (Page 15)
          Dim lights

Cue 21   When ready   (Page 18)
          Bring up general interior lighting

Cue 22   Everyone exits. When ready   (Page 22)
          Dim lights

Cue 23   When ready   (Page 26)
          Bring up general interior lighting

Cue 24   US curtains close   (Page 29)
          Fade lights on US area

Cue 25   When ready   (Page 30)
          Cross-fade lights to prop room

Cue 26   Dance break begins   (Page 32)
          Change lights to fantasy sequence setting

Cue 27   The mirrorball flies out   (Page 33)
          Return lights to prop room setting

Cue 28   **Buddy**: "Yah, sure."   (Page 34)
          Snap cross-fade to costume store setting

| *Cue* 29 | **Stu**: "Bonjour!" | (Page 36) |
| | *Snap cross-fade to prop room setting* | |

| *Cue* 30 | **Brenda** enters with a flashlight | (Page 38) |
| | *Bring up dim lighting* UR | |

| *Cue* 31 | Clunk of power switch | (Page 39) |
| | *Black-out* | |

| *Cue* 32 | **Brenda** falls to the floor; music builds | (Page 40) |
| | *Bring up lights on* **Brenda***'s body* C | |

ACT II

To open: Dim lighting over entire stage

| *Cue* 33 | **Voices**: "Teen Detective." | (Page 43) |
| | *Black-out* | |

| *Cue* 34 | When ready | (Page 43) |
| | *General interior lighting* | |

| *Cue* 35 | US curtains close | (Page 48) |
| | *Fade lights on* US *area* | |

| *Cue* 36 | Music No. 16a ends | (Page 49) |
| | *Black-out* | |

| *Cue* 37 | When ready | (Page 49) |
| | *Bring up interior lighting* UC | |

| *Cue* 38 | US curtains close | (Page 51) |
| | *Cross-fade lights to* DS *area* | |

| *Cue* 39 | US curtains open | (Page 52) |
| | Cross-fade *lights* to US area | |

| *Cue* 40 | US curtains close | (Page 57) |
| | *Fade lights on* US *area* | |

| *Cue* 41 | When ready | (Page 57) |
| | *Bring up interior lights* DR | |

| Cue 42 | **Stu**: " ... really ought to know." | (Page 59) |
| | *Cross-fade lights to* US *area* | |

| *Cue* 43 | **Buddy** looks through drawers | (Page 60) |
| | *Bring up lights on* **Cecil** *and* **Stu** | |

Cue 44	**Stu**: "Van Strander!" *Snap off* UR *lights*	(Page 62)
Cue 45	US curtains open *Bring up general interior lighting on* US *area*	(Page 62)
Cue 46	**Buddy** and **Stu** exit *Change lights to scene change setting*	(Page 67)
Cue 47	When ready *Bring up interior lighting, with moonlight effect,* US	(Page 67)
Cue 48	**Brenda** enters *Increase moonlight effect*	(Page 68)
Cue 49	US curtains close *Cross-fade to* DS *area*	(Page70)
Cue 50	Car speeds off stage *Cross-fade to* US *area*	(Page 71)
Cue 51	**Brenda** marches DC *Bring up general interior lighting* DS	(Page 71)
Cue 52	**Brenda** runs off *Dim lights*	(Page 72)
Cue 53	When ready *Cross-fade to prop room setting*	(Page 73)
Cue 54	US curtains open *Bring up school stage lighting* US	(Page 79)

EFFECTS PLOT

ACT I

Cue 1   When ready   (Page 1)
Girl's ear-piercing scream

Cue 2   Lights change   (Page 32)
Dry ice

Cue 3   **Brenda**: " ... that's what I want to know."   (Page 39)
Clunk of power switch

ACT II

Cue 4   As Scene 7 starts   (Page 67)
Crickets

Cue 5   **Brenda** runs off   (Page 71)
Sound of car revving up and disappearing

Cue 6   **Brenda** leans out of the ship   (Page 71)
*Wind blows **Brenda**'s hair*

Cue 7   **Brenda** snow-skis   (Page 71)
*Fake snow is blown about **Brenda***

MANAGEMENT OF FIREARMS AND OTHER WEAPONS IN PRODUCTIONS

Recommended reading:

Entertainment Information Sheet No. 20 (Health and Safety Executive). This information sheet is one of a series produced in consultation with the Joint Advisory Committee for Broadcasting and the Performing Arts. It gives guidance on the management of weapons that are part of a production, including firearms, replicas and deactivated weapons.
It is obtainable from: HSE Books, PO Box 1999, Sudbury, Suffolk, CO10 2WA. Tel: 01787 881165, Fax: 01787 313995. Or it may be downloaded from: www.hse.gov.uk

Home Office Firearms Law: Guidance to the Police. The Stationery Office 2002. ISBN 0 11 341273 8. Also available from: www.homeoffice.gov.uk

Health and Safety in Audio-visual Production: Your legal duties. Leaflet INDG360. HSE Books 2002

Lightning Source UK Ltd.
Milton Keynes UK
UKHW051117021219
354566UK00007B/114/P